AM.

MW01284876

A STEP BY STEP GUIDE TO LAUNCH YOUR ONLINE BUSINESS.

HOW TO BUILD AN AMAZON BUSINESS AND EARN A PASSIVE INCOME IN 60 DAYS.

LOGAN STORE

Table of Contents

Introduction

Fulfilled by Amazon. FBA.

Three letters. One life-changing experience.

Taking that leap of faith and trying to start your own business is scary. It is a bold, daring move that not many would dare to make. Making the jump from being an employee, to become your own boss who works for yourself takes courage. However, Amazon's FBA service might just make the perspective a little less daunting.

Before we begin, take a moment to congratulate yourself. Congratulate yourself on rising to the challenge and heeding the call of entrepreneurship. Congratulate yourself for finally taking another step towards greater financial freedom and making your dreams come true. It is a decision that not many would be brave enough to do and you should feel extremely proud of yourself. You believed enough in your abilities to decide to make a difference and that is what you are about to do right now.

The FBA process where you store your products in Amazon's fulfillment centers and they will pick your products, pack it for you and ship it for you. They will even help you manage the customer service and returns for these products. When you list your products on FBA, customers are eligible for free shipping and qualified listings are shown using the Prime logo. Customers browsing your site know that Amazon will do the packing, delivery and everything for the product.

It is the perfect platform for the well-informed business owner who is keen on catering to a larger audience group one day. In addition, if you are just starting out with no business experience, this is the *perfect* platform to learn the ropes and discover what it means to run your own business from start to finish.

Books about the topic are in abundance in the market and we thank you for picking ours! Every attempt was made to make sure all information is as needed as possible! Enjoy!

Chapter 1: FBA and All Its Wonders

Living paycheck to paycheck, truth be told, is no way to live at all. From a financial standpoint, it is neither suitable nor sustainable and the stress of worrying about your money running out before the end of the month is going to eventually get to you. Far too many variables involved can quickly cause you to hit rock bottom financially if you do not have any savings, an emergency fund, or something to fall back on if things took a turn for the worse tomorrow and you happen to find yourself out of a job. Yikes!

Thankfully, though, it is not all doom and gloom, since the digital age that we live in has afforded us plenty of opportunities to bounce back, generate a passive income stream and start an online business in half the time it normally take, thanks to eCommerce platforms like dropshipping, eBay and Amazon FBA.

Amazon FBA Explained

Online shopping, a concept unheard several decades ago, has emerged to become a part of life for the average consumer. Statistics from 2017 alone, state that more than 1.66 billion shoppers made purchases online and, within that same year, online retail sales globally accounted for almost $2.3 trillion. That number is expected to double by the time 2021 rolls around. An unstoppable force, the online retail space is set to grow bigger and better over the next few years. It is already showing signs of becoming the preferred shopping method for consumers. It is fast, easy, convenient, safe and they do not even have to leave the comfort of their own homes to get the items they need. No more long commutes, sitting through traffic and battling long queues at the stores just to get what they want. Now their products come directly to them with minimal effort. No wonder online retail is so popular, servicing everything from masses to niche markets and more.

Since Jeff Bezos founded it, Amazon has experienced growth at a rapid rate. It is now responsible for 80% of all retail growth that takes place online in the United States *alone*. By the end of 2019, the e-retail giant is estimated to hold 53.7% of the total sales made online in the U.S. and that is going to amount roughly $325 billion in sales. That is impressive by any standards and with more people turning to Amazon to everything from their daily essentials to niche products you can online get online, this is going to be every seller's passive income dream come true.

There are many ways for a seller to get their goods moving online, but FBA is still one of the most profitable and popular methods by far. As one of today's most lucrative methods of earning an online income, Amazon FBA has quickly become the preferred eCommerce solution, especially for those who have been selling their products on eBay for a while. Managing an online business has never been easier since Amazon FBA was introduced, with the platform helping you out by overseeing all the nitty-gritty details so you can focus on the thing that matters most: *Running your business.* The platform has even made its tagline *"You sell it, we ship it"* to show just how easy it can be to run a business, even if you are a beginner.

FBA stands for *Fulfilment by Amazon* and it is currently home to more than 2 million people, counting worldwide, who are using this platform to market and sell their goods. It could be goods that you are selling wholesale or in bulk, goods that you made yourself, even pre-loved items that you no longer want can still bring in some money so nothing goes to waste. As the name "FBA" implies, you sell your products through the platform and Amazon does the shipping for you. Here is a swift brief of how the complete process works:

- You send your goods to Amazon and they store it in their warehouses.
- A customer browses Amazon's website and when they like what they see, they purchase your product.
- Amazon picks up the products, packs it and ships it to the customer using the order details received.

- Amazon helps you keep track of your order until it safely arrives on the customer's doorstep
- You have one happy customer.
- If there is a problem with the order, Amazon steps right in and handles any returns or refunds on your behalf.

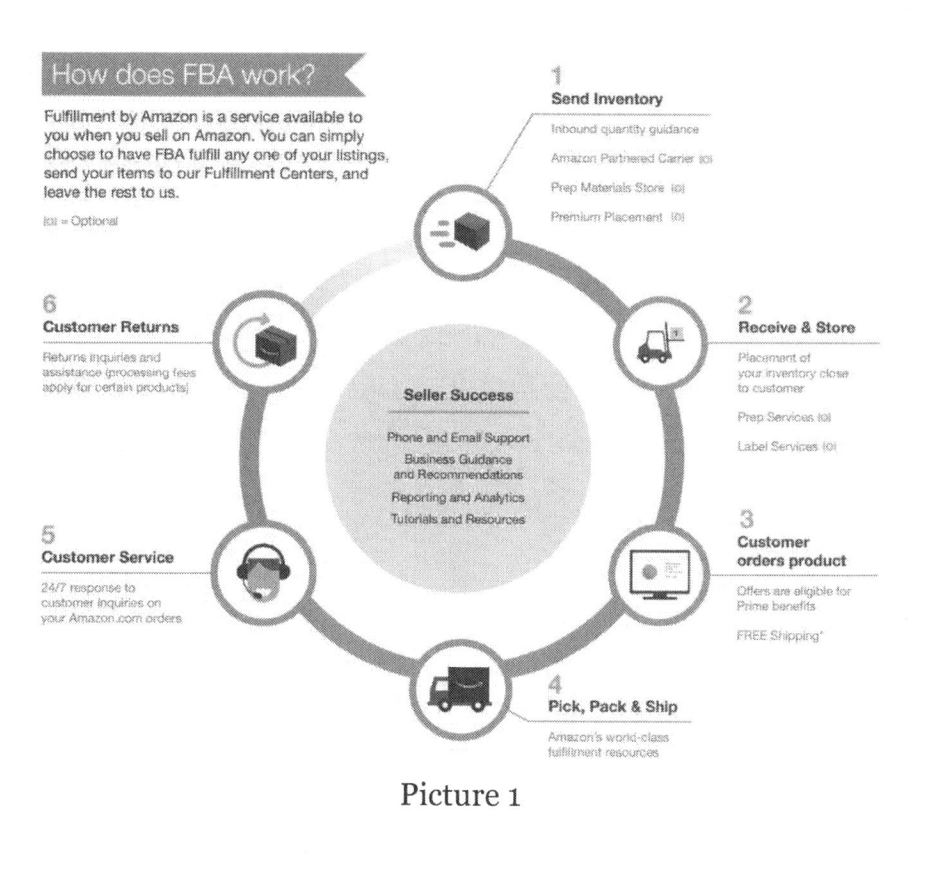

Picture 1

Easy, right? Almost as if the hardest part of your job is going to be procuring the goods. FBA is doing so well that half of the platform's sales are originating directly from third-party sellers, all of which are using FBA to get the job done. Once you have enrolled in Amazon's FBA program, you will be able to reap the benefits and perks that its other members are already enjoying too. Like automating your order fulfillment for example. Easily done by taking advantage of Amazon's advanced shipping and fulfillment services. You will be able to earn more sales when you become part of Amazon's Prime customer tier.

With Amazon Doing All the Work, What *Does* the Seller Do?

With Amazon doing all the heavy lifting, what do you do as the seller? Procure the goods and find your suppliers for one thing, which is possibly the most important part of the job. Without the right products and a reliable supplier, there will be no business, to begin with. You have other tasks as a seller (which Amazon will not do for you), include:

- **Keeping Track of Your Inventory -** Managing your inventory is going to be your responsibility. Amazon will notify you when your inventory is running low. It is your job to make sure that the items you sell are always in stock.

- **Marketing Your Products -** Amazon does all the backend work for you so you can focus on the more interesting aspects of the business. Like marketing and promoting your products. Competition is high in the online retail space and you need to put your product in the spotlight and make it visible to people who want your products. Starting a store alone is not going to be enough to drive sales that are going to require some effort on your part.

- **Pay Amazon** - Excellent service comes at a price of course. You will have to pay Amazon the necessary fees for using its storage and fulfillment facilities. However, given the kind of service you can expect from Amazon, fees are well worth it.

With Amazon doing all the time-consuming work for you on your behalf (including storage, order fulfillment, handling the delivery and returns and dealing with the customer service side of your business), the fees you're paying for is essentially for the stellar customer service, which is available around the clock and for reliable shipping and access to the most advanced and largest fulfilment networks in this world.

When it comes to reputation, reliability and top-notch service, Amazon is at the top of its game. Not many eCommerce retailers are able to match entirely what this giant can do (it is the best in the business for a reason). This contributes to a big part of its success and if you are willing to pay the reasonable fees required, you can be a part of that success too.

Is Amazon FBA the Right Service for Me?

If you have a passion for buying and selling, the yes, Amazon FBA is the ideal business platform to consider. After all, since you already love online retail anyway, why not take it a step further and try to make some money out of it? With FBA, what you are doing is scouring for items (shopping) and then reselling them to other customers. Amazon has already made the job easier for you by taking away the worry about storage space, sales, shipping and customer support. All you need to do is find the products you are passionate about selling and get started.

Here is how you can tell whether Amazon FBA is the perfect online business and passive income stream for you:

- You are looking for a long-term side hustle that is dependable.
- You are looking for extra income aside from your regular 9-5 job.
- You want an additional way of making money online, but from the comfort of your home.

- You have always wanted to dabble in entrepreneurship without taking too much risk that is going to land you in debt.

In addition, Amazon FBA is *not* going to be the perfect business model for you if:

- You are hoping this is going to be a shortcut to getting rich quickly (no such shortcut like that exists, unfortunately).
- You are hoping to make massive profits in a short amount of time.
- You are looking for a quick return on the investment that you put in.
- You do not have the time to commit to doing the necessary work.

Quick Stats and Facts about Amazon's FBA Service

For those who are new to the Amazon FBA scene, here are some quick and important facts that you should keep abreast of. One, more than one Amazon marketplace exists and it depends on where your customers are located. A customer's location is going to determine which Amazon.com store they see. The location will also determine which fulfillment service your customers experience.

Picture 2

By far, Amazon's largest marketplace is none other than the United States of course, which also happens to be the most active marketplace compared to the rest. Amazon's marketplaces are divided into the following categories:

In North America, the marketplaces are:

- Canada
- Mexico
- United States

In Europe:

- Spain
- Germany
- United Kingdom
- France
- Italy

In Asia:

- India
- China
- Japan

Each marketplace's website address will reflect its location. Amazon in the UK, for example, is accessed via *Amazon.co.uk*. In France, the address would be *Amazon.fr*, in Japan it's *Amazon.co.jp* and so on. The location of each marketplace would determine the specific regulations and tax laws, which apply locally depending on the country and region, which you would need to familiarize yourself with before you set up your FBA business.

By default, for most sellers based in the U.S., the marketplace would, of course, be Amazon.com. However, sellers do have the option of branching out and diversifying their products into other regions if they wanted to. The advantage of doing that is you are expanding your services and potentially boosting revenue, but the downside is you might have to deal with higher costs when it comes to shipping. You will also need to have the time to commit to managing different stores in different regions. If you cannot, you will need to have the necessary funds to hire help in managing and operating your multiple stores.

Now, if you are happy just with running a simple retail store with no plans for expansion, then you will not need an eCommerce website to sell on FBA. However, if you want to take your business a step further, then an eCommerce store is the way to do. That decision would depend entirely on what your business goals are. One advantage of having an eCommerce store operating outside Amazon is the opportunity to increase the visibility of your business and products, which means you are increasing your chances of selling more.

Several other reasons to consider an eCommerce store include:

- More options to explore selling your products other than what is offered by Amazon.

- You get to implement various other strategies to scale your business.
- Opportunity to build on brand equity.
- Opportunity to increase your market reach through advertising.
- Opportunity to build a solid customer base.
- Opportunity to build an email list.
- Opportunity to generate B2B sales
- Better flexibility with products if it is your own website.

Benefits of Using Amazon as a Selling Platform

For an online business to be deemed a success, it needs to be efficient and fast when it comes to shipping (among other things). Amazon has already perfected this aspect into an unbeatable process, going the extra mile to ensure that their shipping is always top-notch. They have been doing this ever since Amazon first went live and they have only improved on their shipping service over time. A large part of why customers keep coming back to Amazon is because of their renowned ability to get their orders to customers in the fastest time possible, no matter where in the world the customer may be.

Among the primary reasons sellers want to do business on Amazon's platform is because when you sell on Amazon, you automatically open up to a huge customer base with a high conversion rate. This is something you are not going to be able to replicate on any other e-commerce platform, eBay included. You are able to make more money by doing less work than you normally would on other platforms. Amazon also offers significant advantages, especially for sellers seeking to reach a large and diverse clientele that is ready to spend money online, in a short amount of time.

Amazon has - and always will - put their customers first above anything. The company continues to strive to create better shopping experiences; even going so far as to try to improve their shipping times so they can deliver products *even faster* than what they are already doing. It also continues to work hard to improve the overall shopping experience customers get when they come to their website. When you sell on Amazon, you are selling with the best of the best. The other benefits you stand to gain include:

- **A Willing and Ready Customer Base** - Amazon's power lies in its large customer base, all of whom are ready and willing to purchase products that they need. By selling on Amazon, compared to many other retail platforms, the number of potential customers is more than triple the number of potential customers on eBay. This means you have an incredible opportunity in your hands. The chance to reach an ever-ready crowd, ready to buy online the minute they set up their business using Amazon. Sellers on Amazon can reach 237 million customers.

- **Customer Spending Power** - Customers love retail shopping. More importantly, they love retail shopping on Amazon more than any other platform. Amazon's revenue in June 2018 surged to $81.76 billion. Consequently, eBay reported $17.05 billion in that same period. An RBC survey even revealed that the average customer who shops on Amazon would spend approximately $320 annually. These numbers are very promising from a seller's point of view. It is an opportunity for sellers to gain depth and breadth where the visibility of their business is concerned.

- **Its Undisputed Reputation** - Amazon has a credible reputation. When it comes to credibility, no other platform can hold a candle to Amazon, thanks to its exceptional customer service and shipping. This has enabled Amazon to hold a large market share of online consumers simply because of their amazing services. This is something to keep in mind if you are deciding between eBay and Amazon.

- **The Power of Prime** - Amazon Prime can absolutely increase your revenues and increase the number of customers. With Prime, Amazon encourages customers to spend a little bit more by giving incentives such as two-day free shipping on plenty of Prime products. Prime customers spent an average of $528 a year compared to $320 spent by non-Prime Amazon customers.

- **Absence of Listing Fees -** While some platforms charge fees just to list products, Amazon does not. You will only be charged when you have made a sale. As a seller, this means you can list as many items as you would like on Amazon and then leave them until a customer has purchased them. The slight downside with this one is, the sales fee is rather hefty, with Amazon taking at least 20% of the profit. This fee is even higher if you are an FBA seller but of course, when you become an FBA seller, you are doing less work, therefore it balances out in the end.

- **No Relisting Needed -** A huge, hassle-free advantage that Amazon has over platforms like eBay is there is no need to continuously relist your items the way you would need to on eBay. Unless you sign up for the FBA service though, you are going to have to handle the shipping and customer service aspect of the business yourself.

- **You Can Charge Slightly Higher Prices** - Customers would be willing to pay the extra too, for the sake of the guarantee that comes with Amazon. Amazon, at the end of the day, is an online retailer. Like other retailers, they make their money by selling items at competitive rates. This process contrasts with that of a wholesaler, who charges you the lowest possible price, especially if you buy in bulk. eBay acts as a wholesale market and charges the lowest price. For example, a t-shirt may cost $15 on eBay but on Amazon, the same t-shirt might cost you $20. The reason for this increase is that Amazon sells new items (although there are used options available for certain products too), whereas eBay sells mostly used items.

- **Home of Reliable Brands -** Amazon stocks some of the most reliable brands on the market. As one of the most trusted retail names out there, Amazon and many of its customers are willing to pay $99 a year to be part of the Prime service. If you sell your products through Amazon, your business is then associated with a trusted brand. If you are a budding brand or the average online entrepreneur trying to make ends meet, Amazon is a good starting point. You get to access their large customer base while you learn the ropes of the business, before expanding to sell your products on shelves like Walmart.

- **An Excellent Learning Platform** - Business is a risk, but you can minimize that risk when you sell on Amazon. You can use the Amazon platform to test your target market for the products you plan to sell. By selling on Amazon, you gain access to retail data that enables you to see how your product is doing, what the demand is and what you can charge for your product.

- **Driving Awareness** - Amazon can be a great tool used to drive traffic to your other websites. Even better if you have a social media account or blog. It can be a valuable source of buyer information, which can give you great input on how to sell your products from what offers customers like, what they do not like, best times to open for promotions and so on. This should be part of your marketing strategy, to plan for long-term and sustainable success.

- **Perks of Amazon Associates** - You can take advantage of Amazon Associates services to market and promote products related to the industry on your website. Amazon Associates is an affiliate program that allows sellers to earn commissions through affiliate links. A slight downside with this option here is that there will be a clash of interest on the products you sell and the ones you promote. One way to avoid this conflict is by selecting products you promote meticulously and not burn your business.

- **Getting A Boost in Sales of 30-50%** - This boost primarily comes from Amazon's Prime program. Many shoppers do not like the idea of having to pay for shipping and Prime and stepped up to solve that problem. As a Prime user, you are entitled to 2-days of free shipping on any Prime-eligible products. This, in turn, increases the shopper's probability of purchases. Combine that with the "trust factor", where Amazon has built an undisputed reputation for itself and your sales are going to jump exponentially. When a customer sees the "Shipped by Amazon" or "Fulfilled by Amazon" indicator, there is a sense of relief and peace of mind. They know their products are safe and they are not going to be scammed, which is a very real probability if they were to purchase from an unknown merchant with no long-standing history.

- **You do not have to worry about Shipping** - You would be surprised at how tedious and time consuming the shipping and handling process can be. Once again, it is a huge relief for merchants, knowing that Amazon is going to take care of all of that for them. Amazon is the expert when it comes to shipping and they have gone to great lengths to ensure continued quality service, in the fastest and most reliable way. This gives FBA sellers a wonderful and must-not-miss opportunity to capitalize on that. Sellers get to save a lot of time and resources, which they would otherwise have to divert towards handling the shipping aspect. With that out of the way, you are left free and clear to focus entirely on advertising and marketing your products.

- **You Gain the Trust of Your Customers** - With products guaranteed to arrive, customers will love any business running under Amazon and its FBA label. It is not only Americans that love and trust Amazon either. Customers around the world have been turning to the retail giant for years to have their needs met. It is irrefutable what those three simple words *"Fulfilled by Amazon"* can do for your sales figures. Even if the customer has never heard of you until you, they will be completely comfortable purchasing from you, thanks again to the level of trust that is associated with Amazon. Shoppers are more likely to purchase from a retailer they know without a doubt that they can trust.

- **You are Automatically Eligible for Prime** - With 64% of American households being members of Amazon Prime that is almost 85 million customers who are currently using this premier service. Those who are members of Prime are *not* going to buy products that are not eligible for the Prime option. Having that Prime logo is tapping into the trust factor once again and when it comes to selling on Amazon FBA, Prime is definitely the way to go.

- **You Get Access to the "Buy Box"** - Amazon's "buy box" is the white box, which is located on the right, the same section where customers can click on the "Add to Cart" or "Buy Now" options. If you are wondering why this box matters so much, here is why. On Amazon, you will find two types of sellers. One is Amazon themselves; the second is third party. The latter category is made up of every company who is *not a part* of Amazon themselves. If you have your own eCommerce store, this is you. Now, several of these third-party businesses are going to be selling the same product, with the same details listed on their site. The sellers then, compete to win the "Buy Box", because, with this option on your page, you become the seller whose product is selected. Your product becomes the one customers add to their cart or buy now. 83% of sales on Amazon happen through the Buy Box option, which makes it a statistic you cannot ignore. In addition, yes, you have to "win" this option and it is Amazon who determines who the winner is. Amazon relies on an algorithm, which then determines the seller who will be represented in the Buy Box and for what duration. One thing's for sure, the Buy Box is going to give you a lot of preference as an FBA seller.

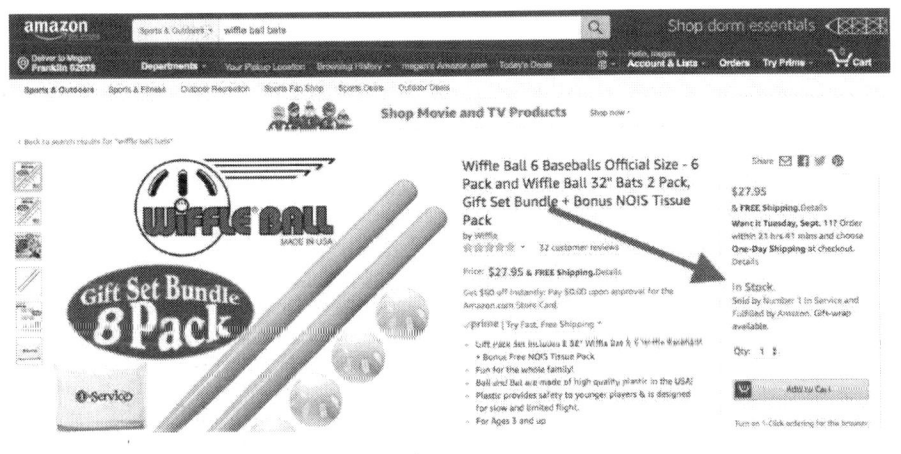

Picture 3

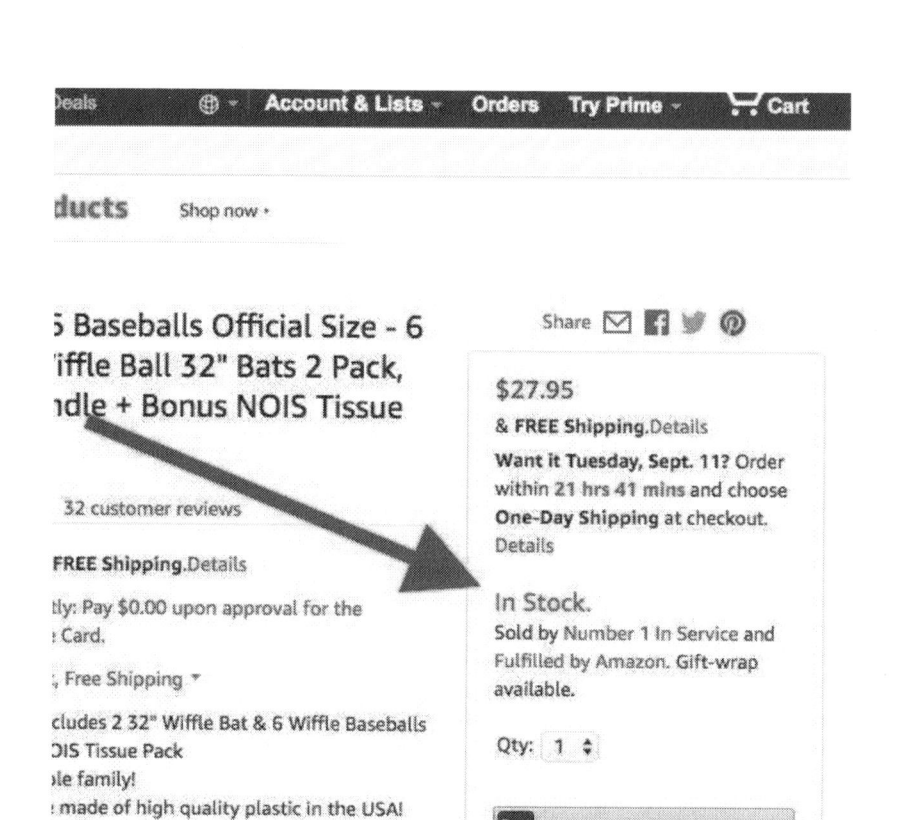

ducts   Shop now ·

5 Baseballs Official Size - 6
iffle Ball 32" Bats 2 Pack,
idle + Bonus NOIS Tissue

Share ☑ 📘 🐦 Ⓟ

$27.95

& FREE Shipping.Details

Want it Tuesday, Sept. 11? Order
within 21 hrs 41 mins and choose
One-Day Shipping at checkout.
Details

32 customer reviews

FREE Shipping.Details

tly: Pay $0.00 upon approval for the
: Card.

, Free Shipping ▾

cludes 2 32" Wiffle Bat & 6 Wiffle Baseballs
OIS Tissue Pack
ile family!
: made of high quality plastic in the USA!
 safety to younger players & is designed
iited flight.
up

In Stock.

Sold by Number 1 In Service and
Fulfilled by Amazon. Gift-wrap
available.

Qty: 1 ⬍

🛒   Add to Cart

Turn on 1-Click ordering for this browser

Picture 4

Another Way of Doing Business

There are times when having options is a wonderful thing. Amazon's FBA feature is one of those times. From Amazon sellers themselves to third party and even direct-to-consumer sellers, there is more than one way to conduct business on this platform. As business is slowly converting to third-party sellers, wholesalers are decreasing as business start switching to direct-to-consumer sellers. As far as Amazon FBA is concerned, this is good news. This means that more sellers operate on Amazon as direct-to-consumer businesses instead of getting Amazon to act as first-party sellers. Third party selling allows the sellers to have greater control, as well as ownership on their business. These sellers also sell on other platforms other than Amazon.

Amazon is also giving its sellers an amazing opportunity to reach a massive audience. For this reason alone, sellers cannot discount the power of Amazon. It is crucial for the growth of their business and imperative to success. That being said, it is not the only opportunity for sellers. Sellers should also look into other platforms to maximize profits, which includes their own blogs, websites, e-commerce marketplaces.

With the operational struggles of running a business as a third-party seller and the competition from other sellers and Amazon themselves, being able to sell on other platforms besides Amazon is a good thing. As Amazon continues to launch even more of its private-label brands, there is concern among third-party sellers in terms of the competition from Amazon. This makes the sellers themselves a lot more likely to move on to other eCommerce sites that meet their needs. It is, however, important to note that these sellers are not necessarily abandoning Amazon; rather they are diversifying their profits.

When it comes to online retail, Amazon is the go-to store. Selling on Amazon is one of the best ways to start your entrepreneurship foray into the business world. As a newcomer, you might be worried about staying on top of industry developments and what is going on in the online retail space. You do not have to worry about that when you are with Amazon though, because there will be new technology and developments and you will always be among the first to know. The bottom line is, there are many reasons to sell on Amazon. With all the advantages listed above, it is clearly the best place to begin an online business and eventually generate a passive income stream strong enough to sustain you.

Of course, as with everything else, Amazon is not entirely perfect, especially where its fees are concerned. However, if you decide that the advantages are enough to line up with your business goals, Amazon could be the place for your business to call home. The best way to see if it works for you is to sell things on a smaller scale on Amazon so you can get a feel of the platform, if its fees are beneficial against the benefits and if it is a place where your target market frequents. It may not be for everyone but it can give your business the boost you have been looking for.

Benefits of Generating a Passive Income Stream and Why You Should Do It

It is not money that is our most precious resource. *It is time.* Time, the most sacred asset you own, capable of tremendous change when used correctly. We all have 24-hours in a day to work with. Yet, some people have reached pinnacles of financial success with than same 24-hours where so many are still struggling and wondering *"Where did all my money go?"* at the end of every month. Regardless of your race, religion, skin color, age and where you come from, only you can make that 24-hours count for something. Once a moment is gone, you can never get it back again and every moment that is wasted is an opportunity that might have been the turning point of your life. This is *exactly why* creating a passive income stream matters so much. *Your time* is going to be more valuable than any amount of money you could ever make. In the wise words of author John Wooden: *"Don't let making a living stop you from building a life"*.

Money can always be earned. You can constantly acquire more money, but you cannot get more time. You cannot expect to be financially free if you do not put in the work for it now. That work begins by choosing the wisest investments of your time, one of which is passive income. It is your best bet and one of the central methods that many successful people have used to get to where they are financial. Passive income leads you to a life where you can make money literally, while you sleep. You put in the hard work in the beginning and eventually you start making money without having to do quite as much work anymore.

Passive income makes it sound like making money is easy. *Creating* that passive income stream, however, is far from easy. You have to make sacrifices in the beginning to reap the rewards later. It is going to take a lot of hard work and in the beginning a lot of time, too. You must be prepared to see little returns at first, but eventually, it will amount to something substantial. *Patience* and *persistence* are going to be your best friends in this scenario.

First, What Is Passive Income Specifically?

It is the kind of income that you get automatically, *yet* demands very little of your time to maintain. Unlike your salary, which is active income that must be earned each month, passive income keeps running in the background, even when you are not doing a lot of work for it.

Active income works differently. Here, you need to exchange your time for money. It could be a salaried job, or a pay-per-hour one, but at the end of the day, the money you earn comes down to how much you work. If you do not work, you are not be compensated. If you want money, you need to sacrifice your most precious resource for it (time). When something happens to you that leaves you incapable of working, you are in financial trouble. With no active income coming in, it will not be long before you start to fall behind on the bills and debt quickly begins piling up.

Most people live their lives depending on their active income. Very little thought is given to generating a passive income stream. These same people are frustrated financially a lot of the time because no matter how hard they work; money never seems to be enough. The rich, on the other hand, live life completely differently. They focus a lot of their energy and any available resources they have towards generating a passive income stream through sources that include rentals, royalties, website advertisement, dividends and more.

Building your own passive income stream though is not going to be an easy undertaking (but it will be worth it). Initially, it is going to involve a lot of time invested and during this period, you will possibly receive no income at all. With passive income, you are trading your time in the present for the possibility of recurring income down the road. It is not an immediate results kind of the venture; it is a long-term one. Why is it worth it? Because once your stream has stabilized, it will keep on paying you even when you do not do any work for it.

There are many ways to create a passive income stream, one of which is Amazon FBA. The benefits of creating a passive income stream include:

- **You Reclaim Your Precious Resource -** You do not want to spend the rest of your life trading your time for money because that then leaves you with very little time to enjoy your life the way that you should. Passive income will give you back that freedom. When you have a steady recurring income, you are no longer shackled by the need to depend entirely on an active income. No matter what happens, you will be able to land on your feet. When you retire, you are free to enjoy your days and your monthly obligations will still be taken care of, thanks to this passive income stream. Having the flexibility and the freedom to do what makes you the happiest without worrying about money is one of the greatest forms of freedom you will ever experience.

- **Fewer Worries About the Future -** The time to start thinking about your financial future is *now*. Not tomorrow, not next week, not a month or a year from now. It is *now*. There is nothing like the pressure of worrying about how you are going to make ends meet to really elevate your stress and anxiety levels. Everything that you do today will have an impact on your future. What you do today matters for tomorrow. Retirement may (or may not) still be a prospect that's far away, but you don't want to reach that point and feel an overwhelming sense of fear, hopelessness and desperation when you realize you didn't plan your finances all the way through. The stress of worrying about finances is going to quickly eat away at your mental and physical health, not to mention kill any hopes, dreams or aspirations you may have had. Having a passive income stream (or several) takes away many of those worries. You do not have to worry as much about your financial future when you have taken the steps to secure it from this moment. Passive income is something that gets bigger with time and momentum, so the sooner you get started, the better your finances will look like one day.

- **You Are Your Own Boss** - Being in charge of your own life and calling all the shots and not having to answer to a boss 9-5 anymore is a liberating feeling. You make the rules, you hold the power and it is up to you to steer your life (and finances) towards the direction you want it to go. You are free to explore your creativity and your passion without having to ask for permission or get approval. You do not work for others anymore; you work for yourself. With Amazon FBA for example, you oversee the running your own business and the success of your business achieves is entirely in your hands. Not having to depend on anyone else is freedom in its own way.

- **You Can Work from Anywhere** - Imagine being able to work even when you are halfway across the world touring the sites? Not "work" per se, but the little effort needed to sometimes maintain or check in on your passive income streams will not confine you to an office the way a 9-5 job would. You can work at the nearby Starbucks or cafe when you want, even when you have a little free time on your vacation and you feel like checking in to see how things are going. Another freedom benefit that comes with not having to depend on an active income stream for your livelihood.

- **You Have Financial Security** - No matter what happens to you or the economy, you know your financial state is secure when you have one or several multiple income streams coming in. If you are suddenly let go from your steady job and paycheck, you are not as stressed out and panicked, as you would be if you had no passive income stream at all. Financial security is one of the best gifts you can give your future self and the sense of relief you get at still seeing regular deposits coming into your bank account even without an active income is priceless.

Chapter 2: The Beginning

It all begins with a plan. A business plan, that is.

One of the very first things an entrepreneur needs to do before beginning any kind of new business venture is to have a business plan. Yes, even when you are running an online business like Amazon FBA. A business plan is always useful and more importantly, it's integral if you want to start your business off on the right foot.

Preparing a solid business plan for your business to stand on, can take a long time to put together. There is a tremendous amount of research that goes into it since its imperative that you get it done right. Research is probably going to be the most time-consuming portion of the process since you want to be sure you have done your due down to the smallest detail with diligence.

There is still some debate as to the usefulness of having a business plan to work with. Not every entrepreneur seems to be sold on the idea, judging from the Babson College study in which 116 new business were surveyed. The results of the study revealed that having a formal business plan seemed to make little to no difference at all, in whether a business was ultimately successful.

This assumes that the business did not seek funding from external sources. Some even argued that spending time on developing this business plan was stifling the startup process.

However, another study revealed that entrepreneurs were more likely to succeed by 16% if they had a business plan. Even more, studies pointed out that a business plan may not be a guaranteed indicator of success, but it did indicate that an entrepreneur who was committed to taking this plan through to the end was more likely to succeed than those who did not have any kind of plan at all.

Ultimately, if a business plan could potentially give your business a greater chance at success, why not do it?

How to Create a Business Plan and *Why* You Should Have One

Let us go through a couple of questions first:

- Do you have plans to expand your business in the future?
- Do you want to increase your competitiveness within the industry?
- Do you have certain business goals that you want to achieve within a reasonable period?

Assuming you've answered yes to any (or all) of the above, then those are the reasons why you should have a business plan before beginning your Amazon FBA venture or any kind of business, for that matter. Ultimately, planning and preparation are always going to lead to a better outcome when you have something to guide your way. Think of your business plan as a compass that is pointing you towards the right direction.

A business plan is important in many ways and here are some other reasons why having one is a good idea:

- **It Helps If You Need Financing** - You are going to have a hard time finding any kind of financing without a plan of action to show. Banks and investors will be looking for something concrete, something to convince them why they should take a risk on you. Essentially, you need to prove why you are a worthwhile investment. A business plan shows that you are committed, serious, that you have done your due diligence and predicted where your income and profit will come from. Having a plan allows these lenders to get a better idea about what your business is, to see your vision from your point of view.

- **It Sets Your Priorities** - Even running an online business, there will be a lot going on. Everything you need to attend to is going to pull your attention in a million different directions. Without priorities in place, it can be easy to focus too much time on the less important aspects and spend far too much time focusing on the wrong areas. If you've got business goals you want to achieve, having a business plan will define what your priorities should be, map out a plan of action you need to take and have a contingency plan for any challenges you might face on the road ahead.

- **It Puts You in Control** - When you have a plan on your hands, you know what is going on. You are aware of everything that is taking place and that gives you a sense of control. You are the captain of your business ship and it is up to you to control which direction your business heads towards. With a plan, you are in charge every step of the way because you know which markets you need to target and who your competitors are. You know where you are, where you need to be and what obstacles you need to overcome to get there. You understand your finances, your goals and your measure of success.

- **Making Better Business Decisions** - There is no time to be indecisive or on the fence when you are running your own business. You need to be confident and you need to make firm business decisions that you stand by. A business plan helps make that process easier because you have got the facts laid out in front of you and your tough decisions are going to be based on which facts will provide a better outcome.

Getting started with a business plan is probably the hardest part of the process. You are staring at a blank sheet of paper in front of you, wondering where and how to begin. You do not need many fantastic ideas to begin with, what you need are discipline and focus. It is okay if your business plan takes a while before it comes together if you get it done right. In addition, here is the thing; you *do not* have to start with a blank sheet of paper either. A quick search online will reveal more than enough business plan templates for you to choose from.

When preparing a business plan, there are several areas of focus that must be included. The United States Small Business Administration (SBA) recommends that every business plan include the following details:

- **An Executive Summary**, which gives an overall snapshot of what your business is.

- **A Company Description** describing what your business is, what you sell and what you do.

- **A Market Analysis** containing all the research information you have uncovered about your competitors, target market and industry.

- **A Marketing and Sales Plan** that details what your sales strategy is and how you intend to market your business.

- **A Business Management Structure:** plan of your business.

- **Produce and Service** details about what your business intends to sell or provide.

- **Funding Details** about the amount of money needed for a 3 to 5-year projection.

- **Financial Projections** with details about your balance sheet and profit estimates.

- **An Appendix,** which is an optional section where you can include any relevant resumes or permits as needed.

Contents of a Business Plan (Picture 5)

As for writing your business plan, these are the guidelines you want to stick to:

- Always research, do more research and do *even more* research about your target market, products, competitors and more. Cover all areas of your business from top to bottom.

- Be clear about what your plan's purpose is.

- Create a clear profile of your company, including details about when it started, the history, the products or services offered resources, audience and what makes your business special. On websites, this is commonly found in the "About Us" section.

- Record *everything* that goes on in your business, right down to the smallest detail. Document everything from the process to your expenses and cash flow.

- Be eager to accustomed and adjust as needed. Customers, the nature of your business and the business environment, in general, is always changing and you need to be able to adapt right along with it.

Amazon Fees and Costs

This is going to be part of your business plan preparation and you are going to need to be as detailed as possible so you know exactly where your money is going and how it is being spent. Considering the amount of work Amazon does for you, the fees are surprisingly reasonable:

- **Professional Accounts and Individual Seller Accounts -** There are two types of accounts available on Amazon, professional and individual seller. Individual seller accounts are usually free, but there will be higher sales fees involved. Professional accounts have a monthly subscription fee of $39.95, but with lower sales fees incurred. The account you choose depends on what your sales volume would be. If you are planning to sell more than 40 items per month, then it is better to get a professional account. If you only plan to sell no more than a few items per month, go with the individual seller account as your best bet.

- **Amazon Fees -** In exchange for doing a lot of your workload, Amazon charges a fee for their services. This is no different from other online marketplaces. Here is a quick rundown of the fees you can expect to incur on Amazon FBA:

- The individual seller account comes with an additional $1.00 flat fee that Amazon charges for every product sold.

- A 15% referral fee on all sales for most categories listed on Amazon.

- There is a fee charged to cover shipping and handling cost too, but the good news is that the fees you end up paying are still significantly lower than what you would pay if you shipped it yourself.

- There is also a flat fee for things like DVDs and books.

- Long-term storage fees when you keep your inventory a little too long at Amazon fulfillment centers.

- There are inventory costs involved too. Based on the kind of products you choose to sell on Amazon, the costs for inventory will vary. It is recommended that you utilize a private label method. It is best to start with just a few things around the house that you already own to sell on Amazon just to get a feel on using Amazon FBA.

Diving even deeper into the various Amazon fees incurred when you decide to go with the FBA program, here is what you are looking to spend on in the categories below:

Fees for General Fulfilment

These are the fees you will be mainly dealing with and two things will determine the fees:

- Product size
- Total weight for shipping

Standard products like clothing items, wallets, bags, kettles and so on are considered standard products. The fees for these are divided into four categories:

	Small standard	Large standard	Larger standard	Largest standard
Weight	< 12 oz.	12 oz. to 1 lb.	1 lb. to 2 lb.	2 lb. to 20 lb.
FBA fee	$2.41	$3.19	$4.71	$4.71 + $0.38 per lb. over 2 lb.

Picture 6

Then you have your oversized products like TVs, microwaves and any other large-scale items, which are also divided into four cost categories:

	Small oversize	Medium oversize	Large oversize	Special oversize
Weight	20 lb. to 70 lb.	70 lb. to 150 lb.	70 lb. to 150 lb.	> 150 lb.
Long Side + Girth	< 130 in.	< 130 in.	< 165 in.	> 165 in.
FBA Fee	$8.13 + $0.38 per lb. over 2 lb.	$9.44 + $0.38 per lb. over 2 lb.	$73.18 + $0.79 per lb. over 90 lb.	$137.32 + $0.91 per lb. over 90 lb.

Picture 7

The heavier your product, the more you can expect to pay.

Storage Fees

Since Amazon is going to be storing your product for you, they will be charging you a fee for it. The price you can expect to pay will depend on how much space your products are going to occupy in their warehouse. Prices are charged monthly and it will be based on the cubic feet that you are going to occupy.

Month	Standard products	Oversize products
January - September	$0.69 per cubic ft.	$0.48 per cubic ft.
October - December	$2.40 per cubic ft.	$1.20 per cubic ft.

Picture 8

Order Removal Fees

In case you need to dispose of some of your inventory, Amazon can take care of that for you too. For a fee incurred, of course, and you will be charged per-item.

Order	Standard product	Oversize product
Return	$0.50	$0.60
Disposal	$0.15	$0.30

Picture 9

While there is admittedly a lot of fees to contend with, they are all low and will end up costing you a lot less if you were to do all the work by yourself.

Amazon's Referral Fee

You will have to fork out money for this one in exchange for having an active listing on Amazon. A referral fee here means Amazon "refers" their customers to your products once you are actively listed on the platform. This fee is generally a percentage taken out of the retail cost, which will differ based on the product category of course.

The Packing and Picking Fees - This one refers to the costs associated with sending your item to the warehouses and the cost of Amazon helping you package your products with their packing material. The fee is incurred over the labor costs involved in Amazon's warehouses.

Weight Handling Fees - You will need to pay the shipping cost to send your products to the customers and these costs will be calculated based on how much your product weighs. Amazon advertises 'Free 2 Day Prime Shipping' for any FBA or Prime product, but *who* ends up covering the shipping costs then? That is right, the sellers.

Preparation Service Fees - If you are relying on Amazon to apply certain labels on your packages, like the UPC codes, for example, you can bet there is going to be a fee involved here too. You are looking at $.0.30 per product.

Why Sellers Are Willing to Pay to Be on Amazon FBA

It is hard to ignore the massive pulling power that Amazon has. Being a seller on Amazon alone can do wonders for your online repertoire as a seller. A monthly average estimates that more than 197 million people frequent Amazon's website and that is too big of a number for retailers to ignore. Amazon is a clear leader when it comes to the e-commerce industry, beating out even its competitors like Walmart, Apple and eBay. There is no sign that Amazon is going to be slowing down anytime soon either.

Amazon is at the top of the proverbial retail food chain and this is one of the reasons *why* sellers are willing to pay the extra cost. Other reasons include:

- **Amazon's Seamless Shopping Experience -** This is a big pull for customers. Amazon has become a credible brand name, so powerful that nine out of ten online shoppers price check a product and compare on Amazon before making any purchases. Amazon offers competitive pricing, reliable customer service as well as seamless shipping. Customers who find the product that they are looking for available on Amazon will more likely make their purchase on this platform compared to anywhere else, especially if they have never heard of the retailer or merchant before.

- **You Can usually Find What You Need -** Amazon's vast selection means there is always something for everyone, even the incredibly niche markets. Customers are sure to find the product they want at a price they can afford, on Amazon.

- **Helping Customers Find Anything They Need -** That is Amazon's mission statement and one that they take very seriously. To fulfill this statement, the company sells as many different products as possible across as all sorts of niche markets and industries where possible, so that no matter who you are or what you need, you *can* find what you are looking for. Amazon's robust platform is home to more than 12 million products, media, fashion, wine, books, stationary, parts and services, gadgets, electronics and tools on their catalog. Amazon's Marketplace even plays host to 350 million products and counting. For sellers, this means excellent customer prospects, but higher competition in terms of getting your product to stand out.

- **In It for The Prime -** Amazon Prime launched in 2005 and at that time, members paid $79 annually to get free 2-day shipping on eligible purchases. Since then, Amazon Prime members have reaped plenty of benefits. These benefits include first-look access to their lightning deals, unlimited video streaming, free monthly e-books as well as discounts at Whole Foods stores. By the end of 2018, memberships for Amazon Prime reached a staggering 95 million users in the US alone. Members not only shop on Amazon but also pay a monthly fee to gain faster shipping and exclusive benefits. Therefore, sellers are willing to pay more to be listed on Amazon. Because customers on Amazon are willing to spend.

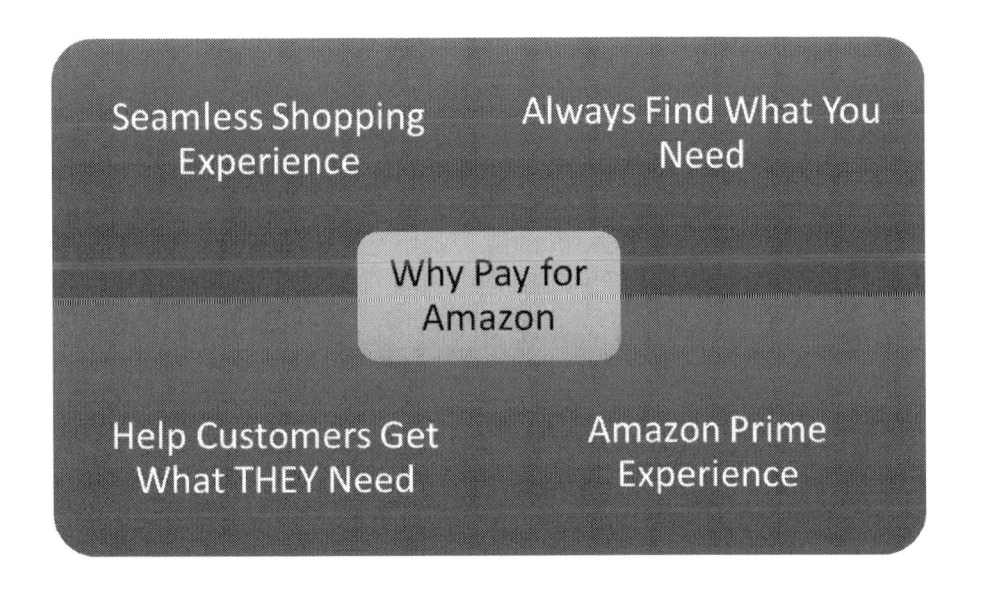

Why Sellers Pay for Amazon FBA (Picture 10)

Being a seller on Amazon is well worth the fees that you need to pay for their FBA service. Having that access to tap into a huge network of dedicated shoppers who are loyal at making a purchase on the platform is going to make a big difference to your business and your profit at the end of the day. If you want to give your sales its best possible chance, this is the platform that you need to be on. Annually, Prime members alone have recorded to spend an average of $1,400 on Amazon, whereas non-prime members have been shown to spend around $600. Your product is going to potentially be in front of 95 million shoppers and that number is just based in the U.S. alone. We are not even talking about international customer potential yet.

How to Create Your Selling Account

There are many e-commerce platforms out there, each one claiming to be the best at what they do. Every platform does have its own strengths to contribute and researching the pros and cons of each platform *before* you get started will give you a better idea of what to expect. Choosing one platform, like Amazon, for example, does not mean that your research ends there, though. Far from it. Choosing Amazon is just the first step.

Once you have decided on Amazon, you are going to have to figure out the best distribution model in Amazon that fits your business goals and needs. For sellers wanting to strengthen their eCommerce composition and boost their business, they would need to integrate marketplace retails into their overall business. Strategy. Consumer habits that keep changing are a big reason why this needs to be done. A consumer's needs and interests also change depending on what they are looking for. This changing need is the primary reason why businesses simply cannot stick to just one selling platform alone.

The biggest advantage that Amazon offers its sellers, particularly the new entrepreneurs who are just starting out for the first step, is its name. There is no other name as famous in the 21st century. Mention Amazon and just about everyone you meet know what you are referring too. Sellers can take advantage of its name to propel their business several steps forward instead of struggling from scratch. This is a unique opportunity for both the seller and for Amazon- the partnership that is mutually beneficial.

But First, Choose Your Partnership

Before you begin creating your selling account, look at the kind of partnerships that Amazon offers sellers like yourself:

- **First Party Partnerships -** You sell directly to Amazon who in turn sells it to the customers. This works similarly to a wholesale partnership.

- **Third-Party Partnerships -** Sellers sell their goods directly to consumers using the Amazon marketplace.

Your choice of partnership is going to depend on what you want to get out of it. You could even opt to go for *both* partnerships, which then becomes known as the hybrid business model. There are many opportunities for sellers to leverage the online marketplace to benefit their own direct-to-consumer (DTC) efforts. Sellers must be able to identify what is best for their business as well as their shoppers.

Something that your shoppers never want to encounter is when they're excited and ready to purchase your product, only to find that the item they want has the dreaded three words splashed across the product image: *Out of stock.* Online consumers particularly want an uninterrupted experience no matter what platform they are on. This means your real-time inventory as a seller needs to be managed across channels efficiently and effectively. The advantage of going with the third-party seller partnership is you have complete control over your inventory and this level of freedom allows you to maintain and create a multichannel strategy. You can move products between platforms so you minimize those moments when you must inform your customers that your products are out of stock.

Understanding How These Partnerships Work

In the first party partnership option, sellers give up their fulfillment control and allow Amazon to decide which products Amazon will buy and how many. Sellers also have little to no control over their inventory, since Amazon takes care of the end-to-end process. Amazon also handles the fulfillment and sellers under this partnership will not be able to use the same inventory to fulfill multi-channel orders. With the first-party option, Amazon is also going to control your product pricing. They can choose to lower their prices, which influences the brand's end profits. Third-party sellers have more freedom in this sense since Amazon allows them to control their pricing strategy.

At the end of the day, with the partnership that you choose (whether it is one or both options), there is something you need to keep in mind. *You need to choose the method, which is going to best amplify your business needs.*

Now, For Your Seller Account

To begin selling on Amazon, you will have to create a seller account. This is very, very simple and straightforward. First, head to the Amazon Seller Central and click on the "Register Now" button. When you have done, all you need to do is follow the rest of the steps and fill out the fields you are prompted to. Setting up your Amazon seller account should take no more than a few minutes and once you are all done, you are ready to start selling. Easy.

Step two of the process, once you have signed up for an account, is to access the relevant tools to get your business going. Once you have set up your account, it is recommended that you also download the Amazon Seller App. The app is free and you will get notifications about the selling price, the fees as well as product availability on their website. Through the app, you can also use your cell phone camera to scan a barcode of any product and the app will show you the price and fee information if you are considering selling it on Amazon. By viewing the Fulfillment by

Amazon Revenue Calculator, you can get details on fee and any items.

There is a hand little tool called the Fulfillment by Amazon Revenue calculator. With this tool, you will be able to:

- Look for any item you desire to sell on Amazon
- Insert the price and how much it will cost to ship to Amazon's warehouse
- How much each product will cost
- The profits you would be making on each product

It is a good idea to run through every item you plan to sell through this calculator so you can see what fees are involved, what your costs are and what your potential profit is. This will help you estimate your profits and expand your business.

Here is an example of what you should see when you head to the revenue calculator option:

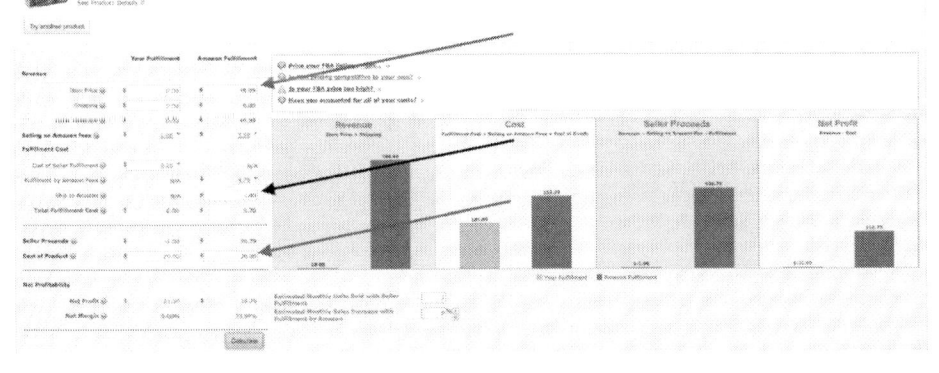

Picture 11

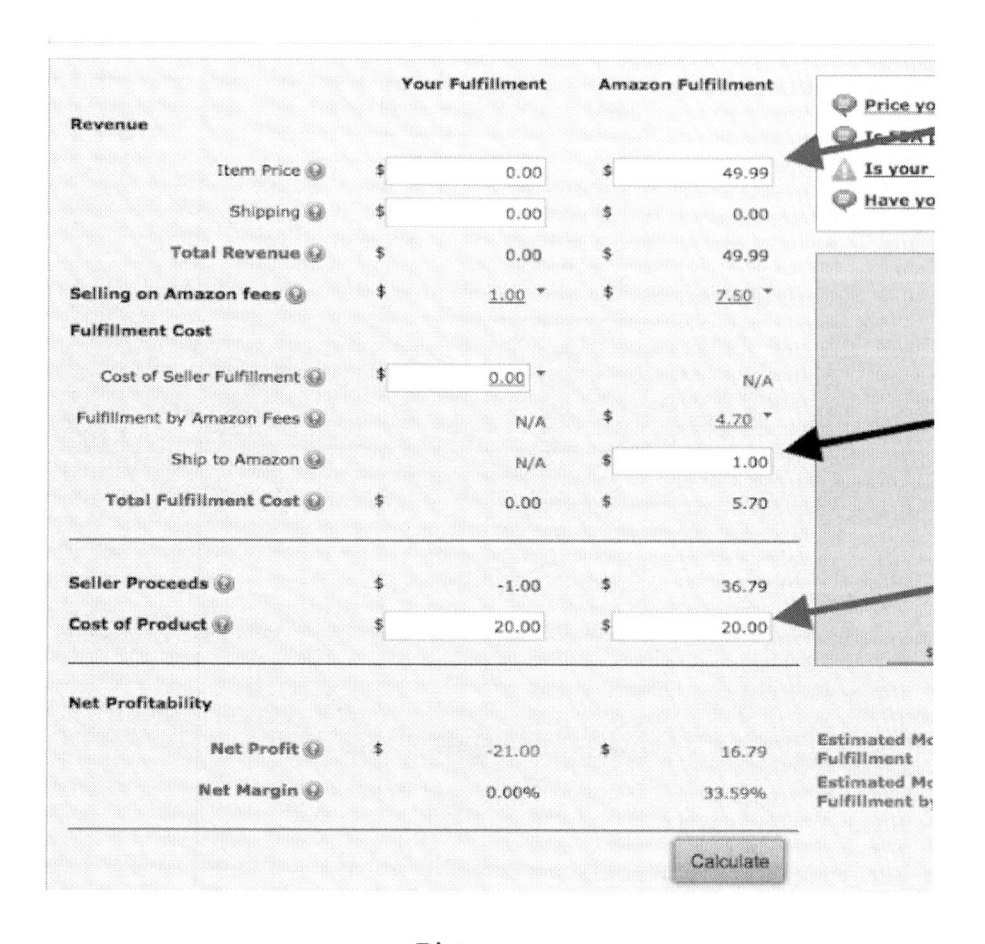

	Your Fulfillment	Amazon Fulfillment	
Revenue			Price yo
			Is your
Item Price	$ 0.00	$ 49.99	Is your
Shipping	$ 0.00	$ 0.00	Have yo
Total Revenue	$ 0.00	$ 49.99	
Selling on Amazon fees	$ 1.00 ▾	$ 7.50 ▾	
Fulfillment Cost			
Cost of Seller Fulfillment	$ 0.00 ▾	N/A	
Fulfillment by Amazon Fees	N/A	$ 4.70 ▾	
Ship to Amazon	N/A	$ 1.00	
Total Fulfillment Cost	$ 0.00	$ 5.70	
Seller Proceeds	$ -1.00	$ 36.79	
Cost of Product	$ 20.00	$ 20.00	
Net Profitability			
Net Profit	$ -21.00	$ 16.79	Estimated Mc Fulfillment
Net Margin	0.00%	33.59%	Estimated Mc Fulfillment by

Calculate

Picture 12

You can easily access your Amazon seller account at any time, through the login page. You will have to go undergo a 2-step authentication process for security purposes. Amazon will send you a code to your mobile device, which you'll have to key in.

If you need help along the way, Amazon's Seller Support is available via the Amazon Seller University site. Amazon's Support page also makes it easy for you to reach out to the customer support directly.

Get Started and Get Selling

All right, now that your seller account is good to go, here is what you need to do next. In brief, these are the steps you are looking to take:

- Step 1: Choosing your business products
- Step 2: Listing them on Amazon
- Step 3: Set the selling price
- Step 4: Prepare to ship your items to the Amazon FBA warehouse location
- Step 5: Box the items and ship them to the designated warehouse Amazon assigned to you

Once your products have arrived safely at the warehouse, Amazon is going to help you do the following:

- Step 1: Verify that the correct items have been sent in the proper condition
- Step 2: Verify that your listings are activated by Amazon

- Step 3: Your seller name will appear on the product detail page
- Step 4: Your item is now listed as available for purchase
- Step 5: When an order is placed, a team member from Amazon is assigned to ensure that your item is shipped to the customer
- Step 6: When the item is shipped, you get a deposit of your sales to share into your account. This share is your selling price after the fees that you need to pay have been deducted.

Each time an order is shipped from your store, you are notified. Every two weeks, you get a deposit into your designated bank account for all the items you have sold in the past 2 weeks. All you need to do is find items to sell and Amazon handles the rest for you.

Let us dive into the details for some of the more important steps of this process.

Pricing Your Products

Of course, before you can price your items, you need to choose the items you want to sell. A good tip to determine what the competitive pricing is now is by pricing your products at a similar level to other sellers on Fulfillment by Amazon. Here is an example of what that may exhibit like:

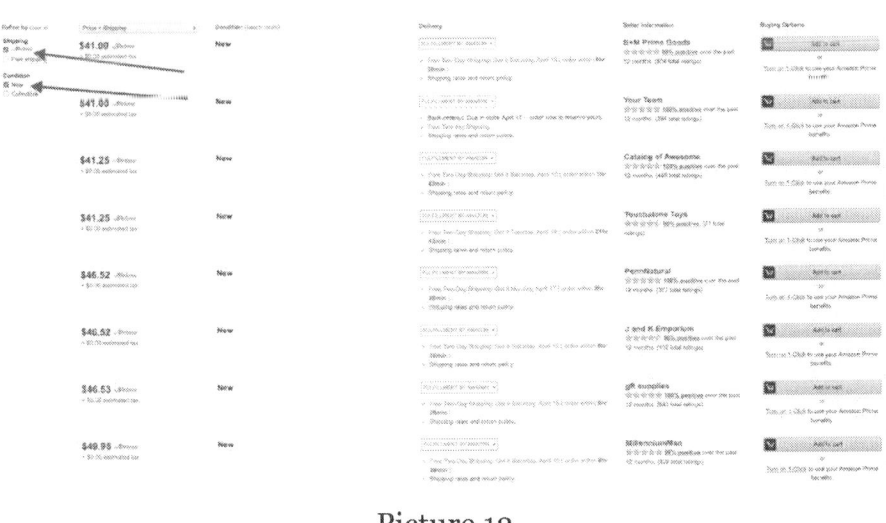

Picture 13

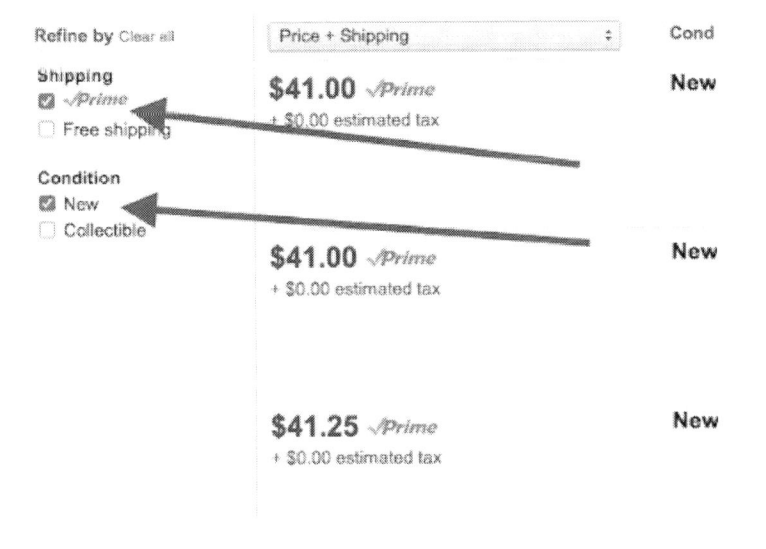

Picture 14

To get to this screen, you need to click the "used & new (#) from" link. Do that and you will be greeted with a list of all the similar products available for sale. The "#" section will be the details about the number of sellers available for that specific listing. You can also choose to filter your results based on Prime eligible or whether it is in new or used.

When you are fixing a price on your product, do not price them lower than the other offers you are competing against. Doing this could potentially cause a chain reaction where other sellers will attempt to outdo you by pricing their products *even lower* than yours. The lower prices go, the worse your profit margins are affected. Low prices are only great news for the customers, not the business.

What you should do instead is to try to match the lowest available price that uses similar fulfillment methods to your own. Your items should be priced somewhere between .01 - 1% higher than what the lowest price on Amazon is. Determining your ideal price point is something you are going to have to experiment and play around with for a bit, to get a better gauge of what the best prices are. This is easier as you gain more selling experience on Amazon.

Listing Your Items

This is the exciting part for many sellers. You are just a mere few steps away from making your first sale once you have listed your items on Amazon. As soon as they have finalized matters from their end all that is left to do is wait until someone makes a purchase. Now, once you have listed your products, you need to then prepare to ship them over to the warehouse you have been assigned to. Do not worry; this is not as difficult as it initially sounds.

What you need to do is go to your seller account and click on the "Manage FBA Inventory" option. Follow the prompts and fill in the details, including your choice of shipping. Detail the number of boxes and units you will be sent to Amazon, too. Follow all the instructions throughout each step of the process.

When you are done with the inventory details, the "Create a New Shipping Plan" option is where you want to turn your attention to, next. If you are sending more than one unit or case, you need to select the "Case-packed products" option too. When you click on the "Continue to Shipping Plan" tab, fill in the details about the number of units and cases that you will be sent to the warehouse. If you are sending 10 samples in one box, then insert the number 10 into 'Units per Case' and number 1 into 'Number of Cases'.

As you prepare to send your items on their journey, you want to make sure that each product is neatly tucked away into its own individual poly bag. Include a safety-warning label too, which needs to be prominently displayed. If you have your own label printer, you can easily print this at home. If you do not Amazon can do this for you for a fee (of course). You will find your labeling options available on the seller's account dashboard. Select "Who labels" and then select "Apply to all" and finally, select Amazon.

Now to choose the courier service of your preference. You have either FedEx or UPS to work with. Once again, you will have to head back to your trusty seller's dashboard and select the "Work on Shipment" option to choose the courier service you prefer. At the "Shipment Packing" option, choose to go with "Everything in One Box", an option, which you see from the drop-down menu under "How Will This Shipment Be Packed".

Measure and weigh your package per depth, height and width. Input these details accurately, remembering to mark the box dimensions as you do. When you are done, click on the "Confirm" button and you will be met with two other options, which are "Shipping Charges" and "Calculate". Here is where you get to see how much you will be charged for shipping your products to Amazon's warehouses. Agree to the terms and conditions as per usual practice and you are good to go. Should you change your mind for any reason, you will have 24-hours to cancel your transaction. If you cancel *after* the 24-hour mark, you will be charged and billed by Amazon. Do not forget to stick your printed labels *at the side of your shipping box*, as per Amazon's guidelines.

Amazon will confirm they have successfully received your products via email, which they will then add to their inventory. You will be able to see this update on your dashboard, although it may take a few business days for it to show up.

More than One Selling Approach

There are several selling options that you can choose from on Amazon, which include:

- **Retail arbitrage,** which involves buying your items from elsewhere and then selling them on Amazon for a marked-up price.

- **Wholesale,** which is, of course, a popular choice among wholesale companies or sellers with larger capital to work with. For wholesales, Amazon is often just one of their many revenue streams and they sometimes have a brick and mortar of their own in addition to what is going on online.

- **Private labeling,** which is an option many already successful entrepreneurs in the e-commerce space prefer to go with. This one requires slightly more investment in terms of money and time, but the upside is, you get to attract higher profit margins. With this option, what happens is you take a standard, manufactured product and then turn it into a brand of your own. In short, you are purchasing an existing product and then slapping your own brand name and logo on it. If you have the capital and the time to spare, private label selling might be a good idea if you are thinking about maximum profit potential.

Approach to Selling on Amazon (Picture 15)

70

How to Calculate Your FBA Profits

As much as you love the thrill of running your own business and being a seller, something else is going to give you an even bigger reason to get excited. *Your profits.*

As a seller through the Amazon FBA program, you need to understand your FBA profits and how to calculate them. Knowing how much you will make with every potential sale enables you to look forward and make better decisions in your business, expand your business and work on better strategies to maximize your profits. Remember, as a seller you always need to adapt and change. When something is not working or could be done better, you need to implement the necessary changes as soon as possible, so your business is always steadily growing and getting better.

Understanding Retail Prices

Revenue figures are the easiest way to gauge how much your customer will be willing to pay for a certain product. As a seller, you will need to carry out what are known as *split testing* on your products in the future to fine-tune your pricing strategy. In the beginning, the easiest and fastest way to identify your best pricing option would be to see what your competitors are doing. You will have to use your judgment in this case to review a price point you think is suitable.

Estimating the Costs of Your Product

Here is where the FBA Revenue Calculator comes in again. Once Amazon has identified your product, the calculator is where you will be able to see the details of the individual and overall fees and the net profit you can expect to take home after the sale. Here is an example of what that would look like:

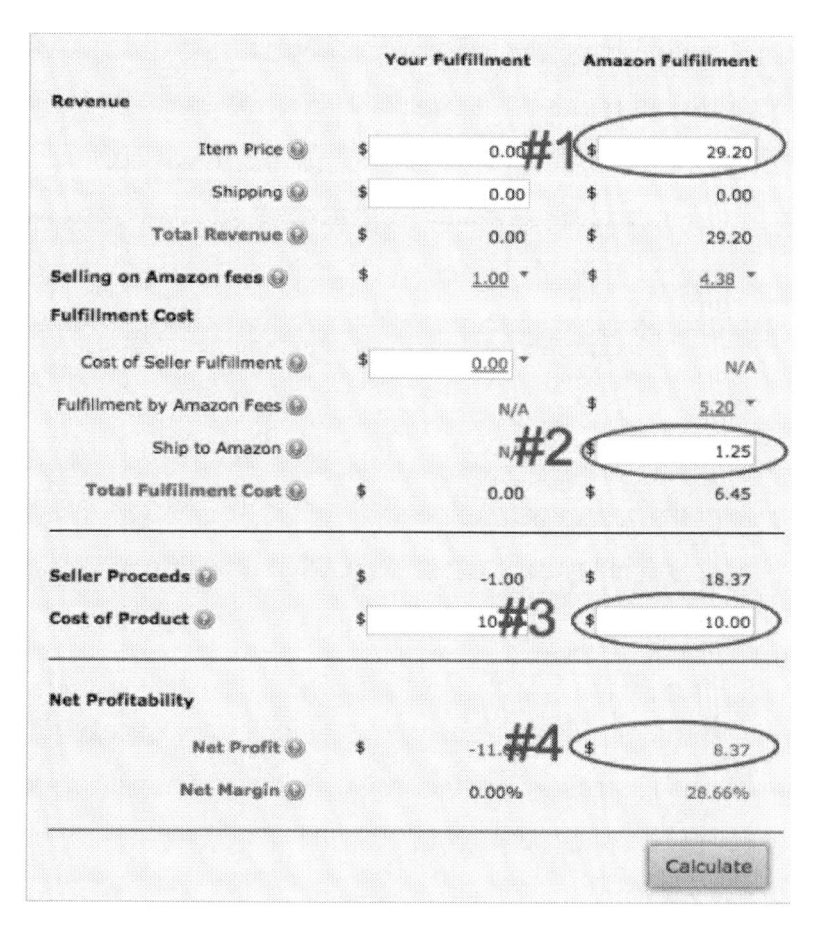

Picture 16

Quick Recap About What You Need to Get Started Selling on Amazon FBA

Just to make sure you have got your bases covered, let us go through the basic preparation that you need before you begin selling on Amazon:

1. A laptop or computer, printer and a mobile phone.
2. Your Amazon seller account and the Amazon Seller App installed on your mobile phone.
3. Your basic supplies like a weighing scale, boxes to ship your items, address labels and shipping tape.
4. A minimum of $500 in seed money to spend on initial inventory.

Why $500 in inventory money? Because you need some inventory to start selling and it is not enough to simply purchase one or two items. What if a customer orders more than two items and you can't fulfill that request because you do not have it? They will turn to your competitors instead and you will miss a sale. $500 is the bare minimum needed to get you going and still have adequate inventory to get your sales coming in.

Once you start seeing sales though, the first few profits that you make is going to have to be reinvested into your business. That is the smart thing to do. Reinvesting your money into the business creates a snowball effect. Let us say you have made $200 in profit; you do not have $700 dollars from the previous $500 you started with. That is an extra $200 to buy *stock* so you can then generate more sales by selling more products.

Amazon's FBA program is a beautiful thing because you do not need any kind of minimum to get started. If a few items are, all you can afford to ship to start with, that's okay it is better than not starting at all. You will be able to increase that number once the snowball effect gets bigger and bigger.

- Manage your expectations, keep them realistic and you will do just fine. You may not be making a lot of profit at the start ($200 profit may not seem like much), but that is still extra income you otherwise would not have if you never started this venture at all. Your business is not going to skyrocket to success and remember that Amazon FBA is not a get-rich-quick approach. You will be to be patient and willing to invest the time needed until momentum for your business eventually picks up speed.

Chapter 3: The Supplier, the Product, and the Niche

Once you have your seller's account all set up, it is time for the next important mission. Sourcing your products, choosing to the perfect supplier to work with, and finding a niche market to specialize in. If this sounds stressful or overwhelming, do not worry, it is not as hard as you might think; not when there are many areas you could get involved in, especially where niche markets and products are concerned.

Let us begin with choosing the right products and niche market.

How to Choose the Best Merchandise to Market in Amazon

There are a few simple methods you could employ in this phase to make finding the perfect products and niche markets an easier task. Finding the right products and the perfect niche market happen almost simultaneously, since they are both related, and it is only *after* you have completed these two steps that you can begin sourcing for your suppliers. You cannot find a supplier without knowing *what you want to sell* in the first place. Here are several key points to keep in mind when you begin thinking about what kind of niche market you want to service.

Key Point #1: Brainstorm Ideas

Always a good idea to make this step the *first step* of any major process. Brainstorming is an effective measure for almost any type of process: finding ideas, thinking about possible solutions, sourcing new methods and even finding the right niche market and the target audience you want to serve as part of your Amazon FBA business. Create a comfortable work environment for yourself where you can comfortably sit for several hours to carry out an effective brainstorming session. This can be anywhere you feel most relaxed in. A home office environment you've set up to your liking, the library, an empty meeting room at work during your lunch break or even when you're relaxing at your favorite cafe with a cup of coffee in hand. Enlist the help of like-minded family or friends, someone you can trust, to help bounce ideas off.

Designate a specific time to commit to nothing but brainstorming. A block of an hour, two or maybe even three depending on your schedule where you sit down, brainstorm and do not stop until the time is up. Having a time-block commitment makes it easier to retain focus. The key with brainstorming is to write down every single idea you have, no matter how impossible, far-fetched, perplexing or improbable it might seem. This is the phase where you just churn out and put pen to paper all the ideas you have got running in your mind. You are not deciding on anything yet; you are merely generating as many ideas as possible. You will be able to sort out later which are the most workable ones. Write down all the niches you are interested in, along with the most profitable ones you know of. There is no need to rush into picking one immediately.

Key Point #2: Picking Your Niches

After you have an idea of the kind of niches you would like to focus on, here is what you need to do to narrow that list down even further. Filter your niches according to:

- **Who Your Competitors Are** - Do your research and consider other Amazon shops that sell similar products. Do your research into what type of products are oversaturated in the market right now (you want to avoid this because your business will be drowned out).

- **Price Points** - Higher product prices, the bigger the potential profit margin. Be sure these are the products that the customers *will be willing* to pay for though. A good tip is to aim for products which are high-priced but low cost when it comes to shipping because they do not weigh too much.

- **Niche Loyalty** - Ideally, you want to try to stay away from niches, which are already dominated by bigger brand name companies. It will be hard to penetrate that market as an unknown brand, especially if you are going against big-name giants.

- **Product Returns** - To save yourself the hassle of dealing with returns, you want to try to avoid items which come in various sizes or styles just to be safe. Clothing items especially tend to have a high return rate.

Key Point #3: Compare and Evaluate

The importance of research cannot be emphasized enough. Always compare, evaluate and research the trends on Amazon. A good place to a source of sellable items online is eBay, but avoid using this as a determining point for your prices. That is because eBay's prices are usually on the lower end. However, in terms of doing your research, eBay is a good place to start. You can use the platform to identify the products in different niches, products in the higher-priced bracket, and the ones that are expensive. These could be along with the $50 or $200 or $500 price point, depending on the product.

Once you have your search results, allow it to show 'completed listings'. Completed lists will show you items in red or green, red being the item did not sell and green being the items that sold. Look at the items for the products you are considering specializing in. Take as much time as you need to go through the list a few times, and identify anywhere from 15 to 20 products that usually sell out. You want to keep your eyes peeled for products which sell at least 10 units daily.

This will make it easier when the time comes for you to request quotes from suppliers, and inquire about shipping costs and storage too.

Key Point #4: Make Full Use of Amazon

As the largest and arguably most reputable online retailer, you could say that Amazon sells almost everything under the sun. Amazon is one of the best places to go to find a profitable niche market, and along with it, what products you should be selling. Finding a niche on Amazon is simple:

- Click on the *"All"* tab, which is located to the left of the main search bar. What you are looking for is niches or a list of categories.
- Find a type of interest, and select *"Go"*.
- A new page opens and, on the left, you will see a list of *"Sub-niches"*. Click on the subcategory you want to view more sub-niches that are specific.

Easy enough. Amazon is also an excellent tool in helping you select a specific niche and product that sells best. Simply browse the *"Bestsellers"* list from the navigation bar on the right of the search bar. You will find this at the top of the page. A simple click and you will be presented with a list of what the current best-selling items are.

Key Point #5: Think like a Marketer

Expensive items are great for selling on Amazon. The average profit you are looking at for those is approximately 20% of your total sales. Making a 20% profit on an item that is priced at $1000 equals to $200 in profit. You need to do more research once again. You also need to identify potential future competition, which are other online retailers who are selling the items you want to sell. The downside with this one is, you have no way of finding out how much money a retailer is making per product.

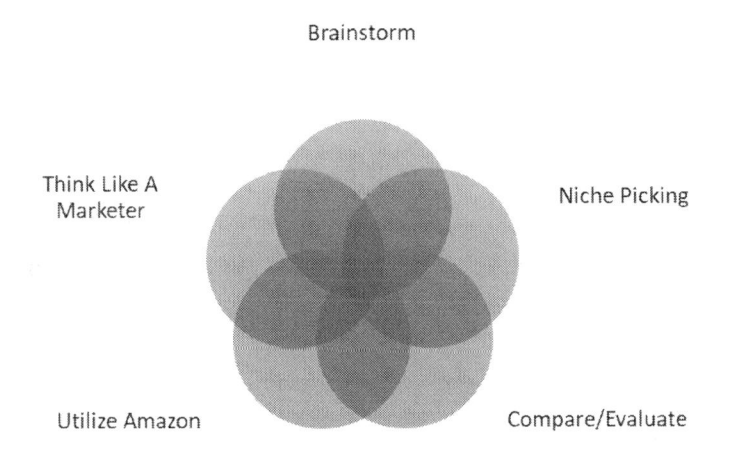

Choosing Your Best Amazon Products (Picture 17)

How to Select the *Best* Niche

Choosing the right niche is one of the many key ingredients needed in your recipe for Amazon FBA success. When choosing your niche, you have two options to go with trending *niches* or *evergreen niches*.

- **Evergreen** - A niche is classified as an evergreen niche when the products are something most retailers would like to sell. Products that withstand the test of time. Beauty and fashion and weight loss are evergreen niches.

- **Trending** - Trending niches have instant profits and surge but their popularity also diminishes as quickly as it surged.

There are several tools you could rely on to help you create a shortlist of niche ideas. From there determine if you can see any niches that show signs of being highly profitable, or where it's aligned with your passions. Tools you could use to source your niche include Amazon (of course), Oberlo, AliExpress, Google Trends, and Treadhunter.

Look out for updated product lists too. Oberlo is one such company that regularly shares updated product lists to ensure that they are always at the forefront of today's most popular products. These lists can also help you determine what you want to niche on. Blog posts with trending product lists should also be within your sights. Blog post titles that should capture your interest include *"Best Buy Beauty Products for 2019"* for example, or *"Must Have Summer Products"*.

Google Trends is something every business owner should use as part of their research process. What you want to look out for are niches that have a stable growth, no matter how slight.

You do not necessarily have to be an expert niche-finder to start, but having some experience in the matter does help. Do not worry too much if you do not have any experience to start with, you will gradually develop it over time. Newcomers can just as easily start sourcing for the right niche if they know what they are doing. Social media is a good place to start about the kind of products customers want and buy online. An example of how you would use social media to determine your niche would be through Facebook Search, a tool that can help you determine the amount of engagement your posts get. You can also use this as a competitor analysis tool to view the posts both your competitors, as well as customers, make. Look at the brands that are within your nice. Search using specific keywords. Your search will turn up based on people, pages, photos, videos, links, and marketplace. When you look at these pages, you can see the number of followers. It will also help you understand the kind of frequency your Facebook posts need to be, which is somewhere between 1-2 posts per day to have a competitive advantage and scale quickly.

Other popular social media platforms to search for potential niche markets include Instagram, YouTube, and Pinterest. It is always better to put your content where it is seen, heard and talked about because this is where your audience spends a lot of time on. If you want to effectively reach your customers, you need to be where they are. Hang out where they hang out. In addition, all these platforms have one element in common. They are all heavy on visuals, which means, stunning images and video reach out to your audience faster.

Passion vs Income

Sometimes the product you maybe passionate about selling is not the one that makes the most money. In this case, you are going to be faced with the question every entrepreneur comes to face. *Should you choose passion? Alternatively, profit at the end of the day?*

The answer to that question is, it is up to you. Some people start a business on Amazon because they want to be doing business that they love. Others might choose to get into this line of business to make more money, and that is the only motivation. The latter group does not really care what they sell, as long as the money keeps coming in. So really, it comes down to what you want most at the end of the day.

In all honesty, every entrepreneur wants to make a profit with his or her business. A business that is not making any profit is not a success. Your best-case scenario would be a balancing act of pursuing your passion and creating a successful profit line. The question is, *how* do you find that perfect balance? Passion should be the one that leads the way first, of course. To balance that out, you should select the items that have the potential to make the most profit *while* still being passionate about them at the same time. That is when having more than one niche on your list to choose from helps. You are still running a business, and the only way to keep a business going for long-term despite the obstacles that come your way is to love what you do.

It helps to ask the following questions when you are deciding on a niche market and product to go with:

- If you have $500 right now to spend on something you want (but don't need), what product immediately springs to mind?

- Which stores do you make product purchases from the most?

- What type of products do you enjoy browsing and interacting with online?

- Are there any product websites or social media accounts you enjoy more than others?

- What sort of products are you obsessed with yourself? Products you absolutely love to buy, read about or follow on social media that you would not mind purchasing in a heartbeat.

These answers will help you get started on your niche market brainstorming session, giving you something to work within the beginning. Now, to then choose a niche which is going to be most profitable, here is what you need to think about:

- What are the most popular retailers online?

- What kind of products do these popular retailers sell?

- Which niches have the biggest audience base?

- What products from your niche have the highest profit margin by comparison?

How to Select a Supplier and Order a Sample

As an entrepreneur, two relationships matter the most. The relationship you have with your customers, and the relationship you have with your suppliers. These two are crucial to the survival of your business, without them, you are going to quickly sink to the bottom with no way of staying afloat. Before you can begin operating your Amazon FBA store, you need to find your suppliers. Contacting your suppliers directly is always the best approach to go with. Once you know the product you want to sell, pick up the phone and call the manufacturer and request for a list of their wholesale distributors. Next, contact these wholesalers directly (again, by picking up the phone), and inquire about opening an account with them. There is no better way to source the selection of products you need more efficiently than this.

Here are a couple of guidelines to follow when sourcing for a manufacturer or supplier online:

- **Google -** The tried and true method that never fails. Good old Google. You are still going to have to research thoroughly though, despite the good job this search engine does. You will most likely have thousands of results for wholesalers, but there is a possibility you may not find *the best* suppliers out there for your business needs on the top 10 of your search results. That is because wholesalers are not very good at marketing and promoting their business sometimes.

- **Don't Forget Your Modifiers on Google -** Keywords like 'reseller' or 'bulk' or 'warehouse' could speed up and narrow down your search results, so don't forget about them.

- **Search Oberlo -** This comes with the convenience of automatically fulfilling your orders quickly and easily, customize your products and even turn to automatic pricing to get the job done. Easily import products from suppliers directly to your online store with Oberlo, if you want to. Alternatively, you could even choose to ship the products directly to the customer.

- **Do not Judge Based on Appearances -** Looks can be deceiving. Many wholesalers have outdated websites. While some wholesalers do put in an effort when it comes to designing an attractive and detailed website, do not be fooled by a poorly designed site. They could be fantastic suppliers, except that they are not so great with the technical and marketing part of the business.

- **Order from Your Competitors -** If your competitors are doing well, they are doing something right. Probably one of them is having a great supplier with a great product to sell. One creative approach to sourcing a supplier is to order directly from the competition. Once you receive your package, use Google to find the return address to find out the original shipper. You can also contact the supplier to find out.

- **Supplier Directories -** A supplier database is another way or sourcing for potentials based on your niche. Some directories use a screening process to authenticate that their suppliers are legit. This is helpful, but not a necessity. Finding major suppliers can be done with good old trusty research once again, especially when you have established the product or niche you want. Directories are merely a convenient method of doing a quick search and browsing through many suppliers.

You could turn to when you are sourcing your supplier's two places. Online and offline. Let us look at some of these options and go through the pros and cons.

Online Supplier 1 - AliBaba.com

Easily the most recognizable name online is wholesale supplier Alibaba. The platform may be popular, but you should keep in mind that Alibaba is your online version of the Yellow Pages. Alibaba is a listing page featuring suppliers but none of these suppliers is vetted by the platform themselves. This leads to some suppliers have reservations about using Alibaba, with concerns over frauds, getting the wrong product as well as getting your delivery late being among the major reasons why they would hesitate. Alibaba does verify its supplier information to some point but as someone looking for reliable suppliers, you should not be banking on the 'gold supplier' badge alone and decide with absolute certainty that they are good suppliers to work with.

When using Alibaba as a source for possible suppliers, always read the reviews left by others. Reviews will give you a good gauge about the kind of service and product quality you can expect. These suppliers thrive; even depend on positive reviews because it is an excellent pull to get future purchases from clients. When you do see a supplier with the "gold" badge, look at the reviews to see if they justify the badge.

In terms of product quality, Alibaba has a huge range of suppliers, but there are still plenty of intermediaries and trading companies that form many bad apples. Research is going to be crucial to saving yourself from the trouble of forming a working relationship with the wrong supplier. There's also a good chance your competitors are also sourcing from Alibaba, and that might be another drawback to this platform since it'll be hard to differentiate your product and set yourself apart. Be a smart buyer and find unique suppliers that can deliver differentiated products at equally competitive prices. When you look into online sourcing, you need to identify the kind of supplier you are looking for. Identifying the right kind of supplier means considering your needs, and finding a supplier that matches your business needs.

Ask for images or even video, and packaging before you place any sample orders so you can see if you have any preliminary problems with the product. You can also try asking if the product has any defects though they may or may not tell you, it is worth asking. If they do reply, then you can negotiate a discount for the defects.

Online Supplier 2 - DHGate

This platform usually targets smaller volume buyers. The biggest advantage of DHGate is even lower minimum order quantities, which goes as low as 1 piece. There are also plenty of products to choose from, and it is an excellent alternative to Aliexpress or even when you try to look for niche items. DHGate offers an escrow service to protect buyers, but this will cost you some extra money on top of the existing quotation.

Among the pros of this platform are the larger variety of product options to choose from, especially in terms of niche markets. In addition, you are not pressured into ordering in bulk if you do not want to. The drawbacks, however, include prices usually being 25% more expensive, and you may end up dealing with intermediaries. The dangers of dealing with the intermediary include hidden factory information, higher prices and even more alarming, the prospect of them doing a disappearing act. It is also hard to establish long-term relationships with direct manufacturers. You will need to be wary about counterfeit and defective products too.

Online Supplier 3 - AliExpress.com

Think of this as a version of eBay, but with sellers who hail mainly from China and are shipping products to customers worldwide. Selling both small and wholesale items, this is a great platform to test the waters with small orders or before you start ordering in bulk for your FBA store. Aliexpress is a great option to start with. However, if you want to build a scalable business, you need to venture out and deal with the manufacturer directly.

AliExpress is a platform where you will find some similar products offered on Alibaba too. An advantage with this option is the lower minimum order quantities to deal with. There is also an escrow service for added protection but of course, you would need to pay a little extra for this. One drawback to this platform is you would also need to deal with at least 25% more on pricing. There is a possibility of dealing with intermediaries too, which means higher prices. It can be difficult to establish long-term relationships with direct manufacturer. You should also be aware of defective and counterfeit products.

Online Supplier 4 - Global Sources

This company started back in 1970, which means it now has more than 45 years of experience as an international online supplier.

Evolving from a media company featuring a print catalog of Asian suppliers to organizing trade shows in Asia, the company began their foray into the online space back in 2003. An online supplier with a directory like Alibaba, their focus and specialty are in fashion, accessories, mobile electronics as well as home and gift items.

Among the advantages of using this platform, there is the fact that the suppliers they highlight have more experience with the export market. Global Services has an offline component, which Alibaba does not feature. The company usually begins with organizing trade shows, which are held in Spring and Fall and hosted in Hong Kong. These trade fairs are a perfect opportunity to meet and build relationships with other suppliers, and an opportunity to investigate the products they have.

One of the most distinguishing differences between Global Sources and Alibaba is the quality of suppliers. Global Sources offers a premier quality of suppliers than that of Alibaba. They come with better experience too, when it comes to the export market, which automatically makes them a better choice. It is always better to understand the buyer's needs. Many big-box stores use global Sources. You may need to put in initial work to build trust. The suppliers listed on the Global Sources online directory also highlight their offline fairs and this further adds to their credibility. Being around as long as they have means, Global

Sources has more skin in the game. With a reputation on the line and more years of experience, they are willing to invest the necessary money and time to purchase the booth spaces they need.

A minor (or major, depending on how you look at it) problem, with this platform, is the limited product selection.

Offline Supplier 1 - Trade Shows

As advanced and convenient as technology is, there are some areas where the good old-fashioned methods work best. Seeing and meeting your suppliers first hand is one of those moments. The conventional trade show is still one of the most popular methods of sourcing offline suppliers, a practice which is deeply rooted in the business world. It is one of the most effective ways to forge friendly partnerships and gain referrals, by showing up in person. International trade shows, in particular, allow you to learn and gather more information straight from the horse's mouth about the country you are dealing with, the business climate and how they can help open up new markets for you. You will also be able to find better target pricing, better payment flexibility as well as better packaging and product modifications.

Attending trade shows is the perfect opportunity to source new products that you have never seen online. Many suppliers out there may choose not to have their full list of products available online to protect themselves from the competition. Attending trade shows allows you to meet these suppliers face-to-face. Suppliers want to see that you are a reliable candidate to work with too, and meeting them in person is the best way to inspire confidence that you are a trustworthy seller after all. When they trust you, they will be a lot more willing to show a more extensive catalog of options.

Regional trade shows are an excellent approach to take if you want to get a quick look and feel of the products that are made in your own country. Instead of requesting a sample to be sent to you, *you go to the sample* yourself. Regional trade shows are usually open to the public, which means anyone can walk around, look, feel and touch the products on display. It is an excellent way to discover new products you may have overlooked online, and connect in person with the local suppliers. When you are new to the business, this direct contact can go a long way in those few steps towards building trust and familiarity.

Offline Supplier 2 - Conducting Site or Factory Visits

The best way to determine the reliability of a supplier is to vet them yourself, instead of relying on a platform or other seller reviews to do it for you. How do you do it yourself? By paying a visit to their factory directly. Once you've found a supplier you would like to work with, and if they are located within vicinity to where you are, it's a good idea to consider paying them a visit and see for yourself what goes on behind the scenes in the production of a product. However, before this site visit can take place, you need to first establish some kind of working relationship or familiarity with the supplier. No supplier is going to open his or her doors immediately to a stranger, especially someone with no record of accomplishment of selling online before. No, you are going to have to prove your worth before you go knocking on those doors.

Offline Supplier 3 - Using Referrals

The referral method is another underestimated powerful tool. Want to find the best suppliers in the business? The answer could be as simple as asking around. Ask for referrals and potential suppliers you can reach out to when you attend trade show visits. Ask your business acquaintances, family or friends who might know somebody. Scour through online forums and social media platforms to see which suppliers are the talk of the town. You will get plenty of feedback (both positive and negative) that will give you some idea about where to start.

Relying on referrals alone is not enough though, you still need to do your research and dig a little deeper into the suggestions you receive. Keep in mind too that just because a supplier comes highly recommended by someone else, it does not automatically mean they are the right supplier for you.

Offline Supplier 4 - Sourcing Companies and Trading Agents

Working with experienced agents or trading companies who have been in this business for a while can prove to be a fruitful venture. That is, of course, if you have the budget to enlist the help of these agents or companies. The pro with this approach would be the timesaving factor and the fact that you will have a lot less headache to contend with. You can focus on getting your business started while the agents hunt for the best suppliers in the business.

The agents and companies can offer you the benefit of their wide network of suppliers. In addition, they have been the years of experience needed to learn how to spot red flag warnings when they see it. Going with this approach helps you optimize logistics, saving you money and time. Sourcing agents can also help you negotiate better terms and pricing with factories. They can prove to be extremely useful allies, but only if you have the budget to hire their services.

Bottom Line

Finding the right supplier in both offline and online channels takes time. It is almost like dating if you think about it. You meet with different suppliers, engage with them and see which one fits your needs. While it takes time, do not focus solely on online suppliers or just offline suppliers. Having a mixture of offline and online sources helps ensure the longevity of your inventory, and provide you with a more varied product base.

Paying Your Suppliers

There are two ways of paying your supplier:

- **Credit Card -** Which is the preferred payment method by these suppliers, particularly when you are new and trying to establish a presence for yourself. Even after you have become a thriving business, credit cards are still the best approach to take, mainly for the convenience factor. Credit card purchases allow you to obtain a higher volume of purchases, without having to deal with the out-of-pocket expenses.

- **Net Terms -** Otherwise known as invoicing. This method gives you a certain period before you must pay your supplier. For example, if you have a "net 30" term, this means you have exactly 30 days from the purchase date to pay your supplier. You can do this either by check or a bank draft. You will need to provide credit references to the supplier before they allow you to use net payment terms. This is common in the e-commerce industry, so do not worry if you are asked to provide documentation when you use net terms to pay.

What to Do *Before* Contacting Your Suppliers

Now, before you contact your suppliers directly, there are several guidelines you need to keep in mind:

Guideline #1 - Get Legalized

Suppliers are not going to work with your business if it is not legalized. Before they will agree to form a working partnership with you, they need proof of your business before they allow you to set up an account with them. Before you contact your supplier, you will need to be legally incorporated with all the proper documents and necessary licenses.

Guideline #2 - Know Where You Stand

A business plan alone is not going to cut it. Suppliers need more from you. Suppliers get many questions all the time from retailers, a lot of which take up their time but, in the end, no order is placed. To avoid wasting both yours and the supplier's time, you need to know where you stand. Do not expect them to empathize or dish out discounts *before* you have made any kind of purchase with them. That is only going to earn you a bad rep, and once news spreads quickly (which it will), your chances of working with other potential suppliers could be hurt drastically. Before you contact your supplier, build some credibility and be definitive about your business plans such as launch dates, shipping dates, and quantities and such instead of giving vague ideas. Communicate any professional success you may have achieved in the past because it can help with your dealings with a supplier. Your objective is to convince suppliers that dealing with you is going to be well worth their time.

Guideline #3 - Have a Conversation

A tele-conversation, that is. Phone calls have a better prospect of securing a partnership with your supplier more than emails do. Speak to them directly first, *then* use email to recap the highlights and agreement reached during the tele-conversation. Suppliers are used to having salespeople call them all the time, so you will not be the first. Often, you will get a sales representative who is more than happy to answer your questions.

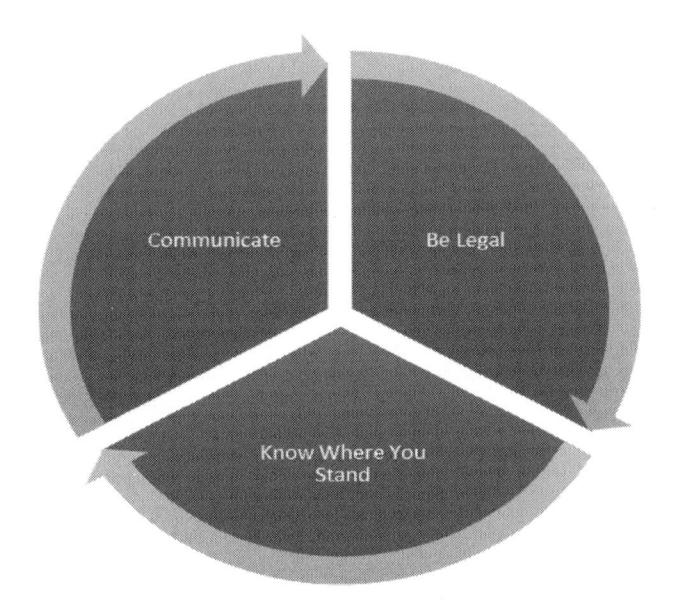

Steps to Take Before Contacting Your Supplier (Picture 18)

Bonus Tips to Finding Great Suppliers

Any retailer who aims to achieve success through Amazon FBA needs to work with the right supplier. No question about it. The right supplier is going to make or break your business, and it is a crucial element to this entire process.

Here are several bonus tips to keep in mind that will help you in your quest to source for the perfect supplier for your business and needs:

- **They are professional, and so are their staff.** These suppliers usually have a sales representative or staff that is equipped with knowledge regarding industry needs, and they are trained to be knowledgeable about industry trends and the product lines that they are dealing with. If you are in a niche product line, calling these sales reps and getting their invaluable insight is an asset to your Amazon FBA business, especially when you are new.

- **There is dedicated support staff available and easily reachable.** When you ring up a professional and credible supplier, you will usually be assigned to an individual sales representative who will not only deal with the issues you have but also ensure that they are there to guide you every step of the way from the introduction, product information and even how to make a sale. A good company sometimes even provides after-sales services, which goes a long way towards developing a great working relationship between both parties.

- **They are located centrally,** making it easier for you to reach out and locate them when you need to. Location is imperative and a supplier that is conveniently located means packages can be shipped and delivered within 2 to 3 business days. Suppliers located in coastal areas often take a week or more to get orders shipped and delivered, which *will* influence your sales.

- **Technology is something they invest in.** Because the digital age cannot be ignored. Great suppliers understand the benefits of having a well-functioning website. These are the suppliers you want to target because they are much easier to work with in general. Suppliers with a comprehensive product catalog online and searchable order history make your life easy too. So, while wholesalers are not tech-savvy, to begin with, engaging with one that does place importance in a good website helps in the end.

- **They accept orders through email,** and they practice good email etiquette too, including having a timely response rate. Having to make a call or manually place orders on the website is a tedious task. Not only is it time-intensive, but it is also cutting back on your resources. When choosing your supplier, find one that makes ordering through email a seamless process.

- **They are organized and efficient,** as part of their overall professional service. Their staff are excellent, and so is their website. Being organized and efficient helps minimize errors, saves time and keeps both parties happy. Disorganized management will only result in botched orders and unhappy customers. This is one reason why reading reviews are important, to gauge the work history of the supplier based on the experience of others.

Chapter 4: Ready to Launch

Almost. Now that you have your sellers' account, suppliers and inventory all lined up, it's time to start listing your items on Amazon and watch the sales start rolling in. This step is going to be straightforward enough, with three main steps involved in the process:

- Step 1: Taking plenty of good quality, high resolution and detailed images of the exact products you plan to sell.

- Step 2: Creating a new listing on your page for these products.

- Step 3: Writing out detailed descriptions and using trending keywords to help push your items in front of your target audience and get those sales coming in.

Amazon once again proves how helpful it can be by providing a detailed instructional video on their website about how best to go about this step, prior to launching your products. It is an easy, systematic thing, so do not worry too much about making mistakes or not getting it right.

The Preparation: How to Launch Your Product and the Steps You Need to Take to Prepare

By turning to Amazon FBA to help you sell your products, you are left with a lot more free time on your hands to focus on increasing product visibility while Amazon takes care of the rest. When preparing to list your items, you need to specify that you intend to use Amazon's FBA program for your items, and select the "Fulfilment Channel" you want to use. To view the "Fulfilment Channel" option, you need to toggle on the *"Advanced View"* settings to see it:

Fulfillment Channel ○ I want to ship this item myself to the customer if it sells.
○ I want Amazon to ship and provide customer service for my items if they sell.

¡ **Fulfillment Channel** : *You have chosen to have Amazon fulfill orders for this item. Your item will be available for sale, when Amazon receives it. Fulfillment by Amazon fees will apply. Learn More*

Picture 19

You will see from the image above that by going with the second option (*I want Amazon to ship and provide customer service for my items if they sell);* you are effectively choosing the FBA program. It is important not to skip this step. If you were to go with option number one where you must ship the item to the customer yourself, your items will be available for sale immediately. That means if someone buys it within 5-minutes of you listing your items, you need to get to work preparing the shipment by yourself (Amazon is not going to do it for you).

Option number two, on the other hand, means your items are only going up for sale once the products have safely arrived in Amazon's warehouse. Once they do, you can rest easy knowing that your products are in the hands of their very capable team members.

Pricing Your Product Correctly

With the FBA program, you will be matched with the lowest price listed by other sellers who are also running their operations under the FBA program. Prime retailers are going to be your biggest source of competition. The good thing about pricing on Amazon is that you can edit your prices any time you like. You could always fill in one price option now and then edit it later once it has arrived at the warehouse.

Pricing is an important sales-driving force, and you want to be sure that you reprice your inventory frequently. This ensures that you are offering your customers *the best* possible price out there, giving them even more reasons to buy from you. Sometimes you will need to raise your prices, and sometimes you will have to lower them, but if you remain competitive and reasonable, you are doing well.

Managing Your Inventory

New sellers often have questions or concerns about managing their FBA inventory on Amazon, especially if the stock happens to be at the Amazon warehouse. Inventory management involves several steps, which includes order volume, sales forecasting, and cash flow. Sellers need to maneuver the process of staying on top of Amazon's search listing as well as promote sales. Here is where the complaints about this aspect start to come in, with sellers pointing out that Amazon makes it almost impossible for them to maintain healthy stock levels, with payment having to be made twice a month.

You need to understand and prepare yourself for the possible problems that come with running out of inventory on Amazon. In almost every selling situation, that operates outside of Amazon, such as through your e-commerce site, for example, being out of stock means that you lose sales for a specific item at a specific time. This is the biggest problem you are going to encounter with out of stock items, but that is pretty much it. Being out of stock on Amazon, however, is a completely different story. Completely running out of inventory could have some serious negative long-term implications, to say the least. Your future sales might be affected when your rankings drop on the search listings, which spells disaster for you if you are selling a fast-moving consumer goods item. Overall, three things happen, when you run out of stock on Amazon:

Problem 1 - Loss of sales and loss of income. You cannot sell what you do not have stock of, and you run the risk of driving your customer straight to the arms of your competitors when you cannot give them what they want. Running out of inventory is going to affect you on Amazon more so than any other eCommerce platform. When you run out of stock on Amazon, there is no back-ordering option for your customers to turn to. When you are out of stock, your listings plummet.

Meanwhile, sales for the product you are selling will continue to thrive on your competitor's page. Until you have your products back in stock, you are not going to be making any kind of sale and your listings are going to suffer because of it. This is different when you are selling on your own website because you are in control over there. You still have the power to receive and process backorders, and your listings do not get affected. On your own platform, you can keep your customers up to date about when they can expect their product to arrive once it has been replenished. No such option on Amazon, unfortunately.

It is possible to cheat the system on Amazon to your advantage by prolonging the order process for items that are still in stock, especially if you know that new stock is already on the way. However, this could potentially backfire two ways:

- If for some reason your stock arrival is delayed, you will end up with orders on your hands that you have no way of fulfilling. Longer arrival times are going to affect your rating as a seller.

- Amazon shoppers have grown accustomed to waiting for a maximum of 3-days for their delivery (unless it is arriving from overseas). Extending your order process could cause them to turn elsewhere for their products if they are not willing to wait that long, which is also going to affect your ratings as a seller.

Problem 2 - No Stock Means Lower Rankings. Experiencing out of stock situations once or twice in a period of several years is not too bad. Going out of stock regularly, however, is bad for business (for obvious reasons), regardless of whether you are on Amazon or not. A lack of inventory affects your search results significantly. The Amazon algorithm depends on a variety of factors when they calculate search engine listing results, and among the most important criteria, the algorithm considers would, of course, be product availability. When you are out of stock for a specific product, your listings will not show up when shoppers search. If you are out of stock so often, your listings are affected and as a seller, this means your shop is knocked down in the search rankings, whether there is stock on hand or not.

If you sell unique items that have less competition, going out of stock occasionally may not affect your search results as much. But if you sell a product with a huge number of competitors, then once you start ranking lower for search results, it is hard to get back to the top again, regardless whether you've restocked or not. No sales equate to no new product and seller reviews. Reviews are the number one reason shoppers want to buy from you. The deciding point about whether they give you their money, or go elsewhere instead. When you are not making enough sales, your product reviews are affected when there are no new or recent reviews from shoppers. Ratings and reviews are extremely important to sellers on Amazon. It is your lifeline to stay afloat and keep up with the competition. When you have new reviews, your search results are amplified, and you are at the top of the search result rankings. You increase your chances of attracting new buyers, which convert to more sales. A zero Amazon inventory literally means no new reviews and no rating opportunities. For any seller, it is important to have smart inventory management on both offline and online applications. For Amazon sellers, the price to pay is detrimental when stocks run out.

Keeping Track of Inventory

Amazon has provided sellers with inventory management tools that help you keep track of specific information that is important to your business. You do have the option of using third-party systems to help you manage your inventory, synchronizing the data to your Seller Central dashboard too. Even if you do choose to use a third-party source, it is still important to know the data and information given to you by Amazon. You can access your inventory data by going to the *Manage Inventory* option, as per the image below:

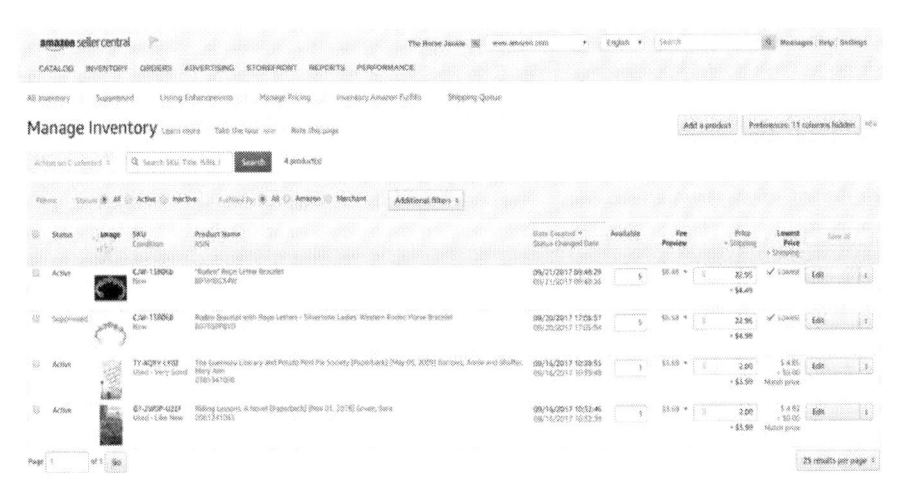

Picture 20

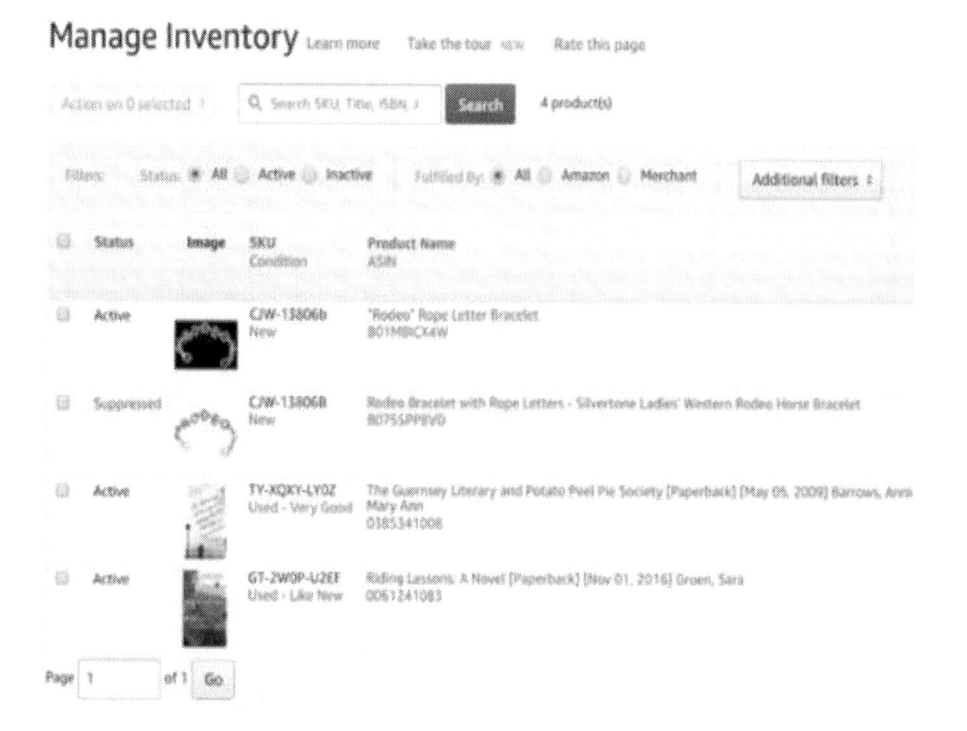

Picture 21

You will be presented with an overview of the relevant and important data for your products and listings. You will be able to make the necessary basic adjustments to the inventory manually. The adjustments you can make include:

- Price revisions
- Viewing active, inactive, and suppressed listings
- Changing the quantity of stock on hand
- Tracking FBA shipments at every stage

- Adding a product to inventory
- Viewing sellers for other products

Amazon's inventory management tool allows you to seamlessly manage larger inventories too, allowing you to quickly change, revise and update your bulk upload or connect your third-party software to manage it. Your activity on the inventory manager is constantly tracked in your connected Seller Central, and you can always view it to get an overview. It is not just a tool that allows you to see a list of your products- it also comes with useful information for you to sell better. It is a powerful tool for the seller, and if you are selling on Amazon FBA for the first time, you should make full use of this feature as you learn the ropes.

Amazon's Selling Coach, for example, is a handy feature that enables you to review the sales trends your product goes through, *and* see the estimate projections given by Amazon. The personalized recommendations on the Selling Coach feature will help you enhance your sales performance with the valuable information and insight you gain from this tool. Information is the key to accurately forecasting your sales data based on inventory purchases. You will get alerts on low stocks to your email or directly to your app, and using this information, you will know when you need to reorder based on the lead times you have set for each product. With the help of this feature, you will be able to minimize the dreaded zero stock status, and avoid any loss in sales and subsequently, lower search rankings. Before you subscribe or pay for third-party apps, it is always good to stick and explore Amazon's Selling Coach and Seller Central and get to know its capabilities.

Planning Your Inventory Orders

As a seller, it is your responsibility to plan for enough inventory in stock to fulfill your product orders between your shipments. However, alas, if only it were that easy and as straightforward as it sounds. The reality of the situation is, inventory managers always must contend with unpredictable challenges such as raw material shortages, supplier schedules, weather issues as well as sales fluctuations. These challenges are referred to as the *"What if"* scenarios, and it is factored into the inventory order lead times as well as inventory forecasting when they place orders with their suppliers.

There are two things which can help you better plan and manage your inventory. Inventory order lead-time, and inventory forecasting.

- **Inventory order lead-time** is essentially the time your inventory takes to arrive in your location once you have placed the order. This process is straightforward- when you order new stock, you need to give enough time for it to arrive before your current stock runs out. You need to know your supplier's lead times too, as this helps buyers manage two inventory challenges, which are not ordering enough and ordering too late. Being aware of your lead times prevents you from ordering excessive stock, and you will become a better judge of time based on how often you need to order your stock to cover your orders.

Ordering too late also presents another potential problem, which ultimately leads to having no inventory in your store before your new stock comes. You can easily prevent or minimize these problems by always tracking and checking your levels of inventory and your sales volume so that it has a healthy balance against your inventory lead times. This is the reason why Amazon Selling Coach is an extremely useful tool to have. It gives you low-inventory alerts so you have time to reorder from your suppliers. The inventory alerts are created based on the lead times you have entered for each product and the sales volume that is tracked by Amazon. With the Amazon Selling Coach on your side, the inventory orders you make are based on solid data- not unnecessary guesswork.

- **Forecasting your inventory** is another approach to take when planning for and predicting the amount of inventory you need when you get ready to place your order. The forecasts are based on your reordering quantities versus your sales trend. Amazon Selling Coach helps you forecast your inventory reorder with figures based on your actual Amazon sales as well as inventory levels. You will need to apply your own experience and intuition too when you place orders based on these forecasted numbers. This includes taking into account trends, holidays and seasonal demand that could affect your stocks. Consider all of this when you forecast your numbers, together with lead times when you make your decisions.

Purchasing Your Inventory

Getting started with an Amazon FBA store is not going to cost as much as it would if you had to start a brick and mortar from scratch, paying for the rental of a premise and a salary for any employees, you hire, but it is still going to cost something. The cost is incurred when you need to purchase your inventory. Many sellers on Amazon consider the zero-stock inventory problem that they are faced with to be directly linked to the payout policies that Amazon enforces. Amazon has a 14-day payout policy, so sellers are paid at least 2 times each month. Where cash flow is concerned, it is a problem to a business that is still in its initial stages of growth. It is a problem because for startup businesses, it is difficult to maintain a healthy inventory, and it is a problem to manage it in the most cost-efficient way.

When Amazon sellers have no control over their cash flow, it makes it difficult to work on real-time inventory sourcing opportunities. With no cash to move around quickly enough, they cannot take advantage of some supplier benefits like early discounts or prepayment options for example. They cannot make purchases quickly enough when they need to in order to keep up with the demand, and without being able to manage their cash flow as efficiently as they should be doing, it is easy for sellers to find themselves strapped for cash. Even more so when they are new.

That is a little something you need to know before you begin your FBA venture, and if you do not want to find yourself dealing with these cash flow conundrums, you have options to choose from:

- **The Payability Option -** Which is the easiest method of turning sales into a daily profit. It is not a credit card, and it is not a loan. Instead, the American FinTech company is here to provide financial solutions to digital retailers just like you, by giving you a service, which enables you to track your Amazon sales, and the daily deposit revenues that are happening in your bank account. With Payability, instead of waiting two weeks per payment from Amazon, you can turn that into everyday deposits, which allow you better control over your cash flow.

- **The Credit Card Option -** If you need inventory fast and you can't afford to wait for your payout from Amazon, credit cards are your fall back option. It is advisable that you use this sparingly though because credit card charges can quickly stack up, as we all know too well. The interest costs of carrying this balance forward can take a huge cut out of your clean profits. If you must go for a credit card, make sure you watch your balance carefully and are not carried away. However, you can pair your credit cards with Payability, which can help you maintain your balances with Payability's everyday payout.

- **The Loan or Lines of Credit Option -** This is one alternative to quickly funding the inventory you need. These options have one advantage over credit cards, which is a much lower interest rate. The downside to this though would be that it could be difficult to acquire a loan or direct line of credit, especially when you are a startup with no previous record of accomplishment. To secure these options, you will have to provide your tax documents and balance sheets, together with a statement of income before your loan is approved. Loans and lines of credit are generally granted *only after* you have logged in the adequate amount of time needed in a business. One more setback is that credit lines and loans are easily spent but hard to pay back. They are best suited for businesses that have an established record of profits.

- **The Amazon Lending Option -** Works like a small business loan option that helps Amazon sellers get the money they need to make their inventory purchases. However, just like the option above, you need to be an established seller to qualify for this option. The loan amount you get with this option will mirror your running sales volume on Amazon. Another thing is that when you purchase inventory, it is only inventory on Amazon. If you rely on this as your source of funding, you cannot use this to fund business expenses outside of Amazon. Amazon Loans are also applied to sellers by invitation, and you will not be able to apply unless you get an invitation from Amazon.

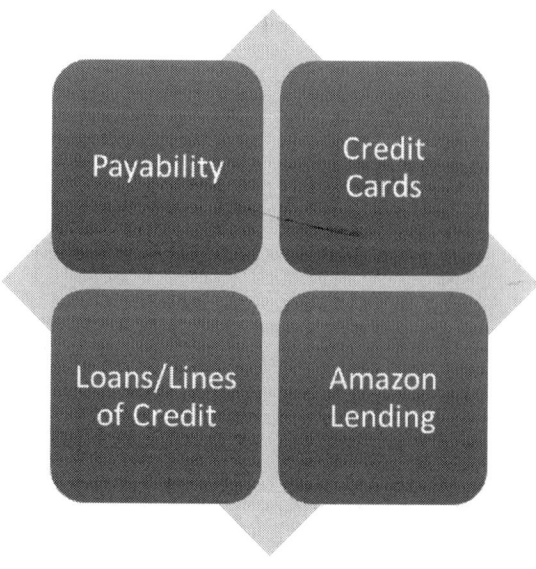

Alternative Financing Options for Amazon Inventory (Picture 22)

Most sellers use a combination of these various funding methods and options to help with their inventory when needed.

Other Tools to Help You Manage Your Inventory

Amazon has become such a popular online retail choice that it is only natural that its presence has led to other tools and software being developed just to make the life of a seller easier. Besides Amazon Seller Central, you will find no shortage of other third-party apps and tools which are free to use that can help you manage your inventory too. Apps are, of course, the preferred choice since it allows you to conveniently access what you need on the go through your mobile phone. Amazon has their own suite of apps already that helps you efficiently manage your inventory if you prefer to go with just one option alone.

The apps that you use will depend on the level of inventory purchasing and selling you plan to do. Multichannel sellers, for example, need apps that will make it easier for them to track their sales on Amazon, eBay, Walmart and perhaps even their own website. Sellers sometimes turn to third-party apps to help with inventory management when Amazon's suite of management tools is not enough to get the job done. If you do find later on that you might need a third-party app to make operations more efficient and convenient for you, a quick search online will reveal all the available options that you can choose from based on your needs.

The bottom line when it comes to inventory management on Amazon is that success is going to depend on several factors. This includes how you fulfill your orders, how you sell them on Amazon, where you sell them besides Amazon, and how well you manage your cash flow. These are all factors, which influence the decisions you make on how best to manage your inventory. Sellers on Amazon have different needs when it comes to inventory, for example, a seller moving a few products has different preferences compared to a seller who is multichannel and needs to stock and reorder products in bigger volumes.

It is important that you understand the issues you face when you allow your Amazon inventory to run out no matter what sales model you use. You need to prevent this from happening and knowing how is crucial.

Marketing and Advertising Your Products

With many of the online retail aspects these days incorporating automation into their process, it is easier for sellers to find the free time they need to focus on branding and marketing their products, not to mention working on optimizing your site. From your logo to the look and feel of your website, right down to the images and product description you use, you want your selling page to sync and flow smoothly together.

The two most effective ways to get your products out there noticed is to market and advertise consistently. You need to stand out against millions of other products from your competitors who are also vying for the attention of your customers. To successfully set yourself apart, you need to use as many viable platforms as possible, like creating your own website, writing a blog and using Facebook to advertise.

Does Blogging Help with Marketing and Advertising?

Blogs are an essential marketing component that can go a long way towards helping your online store. Blogging regularly about your products is going to increase your SEO rankings, and build your brand's reputation among your target customers. A blog can tell the story behind your company, your products and why they can make a difference, which makes it easier for customers to relate to your business. Having your blog gives your customers yet another option to reach out and connect with you through a channel other than your FBA store.

Your blog has the potential to influence your SEO rankings too, and they are not that difficult to set up. WordPress and BlogSpot have plenty of ready-to-go, easy-to-build blog templates to choose from with easy and customizable features that allow you to personalize your platform just the way you like it. Use your blog as a platform to write, edit and publish even more detailed and in-depth content about the products that you're selling on FBA, and don't forget to link the content back to your store.

How to Improve Your Amazon Ranking

To really boost your rankings so you give your products the best possible chance of getting in front of target audiences who are willing and ready to buy, you need to do two things:

- One, as we have already established above, is to take high-quality pictures of your products (think different angles and details) for your marketing and advertising.

- Two, craft product descriptions that are well written and optimized for SEO (Search Engine Optimization).

If you have a great product, you need to let people know about it. Marketing and advertising alone are not going to cut it though; you still need to combine that with keyword-enriched content to accompany your stellar images. Your images will catch your customers' eye, but it is your description that is going to convince them that they should not wait a moment longer to make the purchase. Before you begin designing your content though, whether for Amazon, your website or on any other platform, you may be selling on, there is a couple of things you need to be clear about:

- Who you are writing for (who is the target audience)?

- What details are you focusing on in your description (highlight the benefits)?

- What is the story behind the product that you are trying to sell?

- Is the language you are using easy and natural enough to read?

- Are you using enough keywords in your content to optimize it for detection by search engines and Amazon SEO?

That last bit about Amazon's SEO is particularly important since it is going to be the deciding factor as to whether your products are consistently listed on the first one or two pages of Amazon's search results, or the back-end pages that hardly anyone ever bothers clicking on. You need to increase your store's visibility, and you need effective methods to do it.

Amazon SEO - Optimizing Your Listings

Amazon's SEO works the same way other search engines do. The more people search for and click on a type of product, the higher its rank is going to be with time. Organic ranks that do well have a much better chance of being found, which of course means the potential for sales rises alongside that growth. One method to increase the visibility of the products that you are selling on

Amazon is to invest in Amazon Ads, which is a useful tool to help you search for new customers. It is not an ideal long-term option though since what you want to aim for is organically high rankings. The return on investment for organic rankings is going to always beat that of Amazon Ads on any given day.

Each product page that you create on your site needs to be supported by research. This is the reason why keyword research is important when it comes to SEO. Before you optimize your page, you must know the keywords that are used to search for your type of product and what attracts the most traffic. As a site owner who also runs an Amazon business, you need to understand the best unique keywords and phrases used for your products based on:

- **Relevance -** Tools like Google Search Console make quick work of identifying the top queries on the internet, while Unamo SEO is perfect for sizing up the competition. Keywordtool.io can be used to gain insight into consumer behavior and trends, while Google's Keyword Planner helps you find product page keywords that you can target. It is all about relevance.

- **Descriptions -** Your product names are going to have an impact on its relevance and search rankings. Use keywords that are going to help you create unique, yet descriptive names for your products, as long as they remain to-the-point and include descriptions that your customers will want to know about your product. The easiest way to do this is to do a Google search of the product you are selling and see the other types of description and product names, which are being used on popular pages. Product descriptions are extremely valuable with SEO but only when it is value-added. Your product descriptions that your customers want to know about include information about the product's key features and specifications, major features, and value. You can also include even more details like model numbers, keyword variation, and brand name.

*Important Reminder
Never copy and paste content directly from the manufacturer. Your content needs to be unique.

To improve your organic search results, you are going to have to turn to <u>Keyword Tool for Amazon</u> to help you out. Operated by Amazon directly, this is the tool you want to use for your Amazon SEO rankings to search for all the high-volume and relevant keywords that match your product.

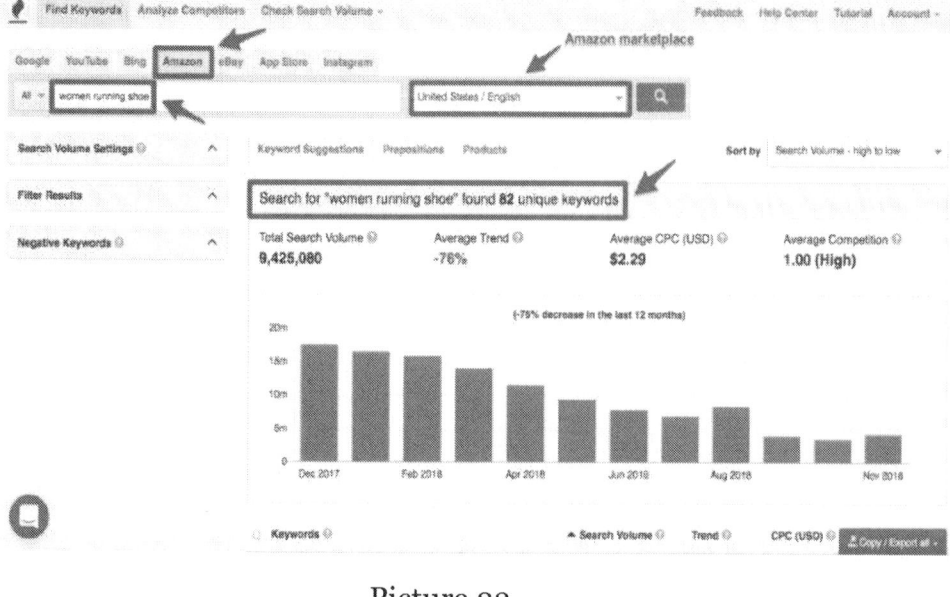

Picture 23

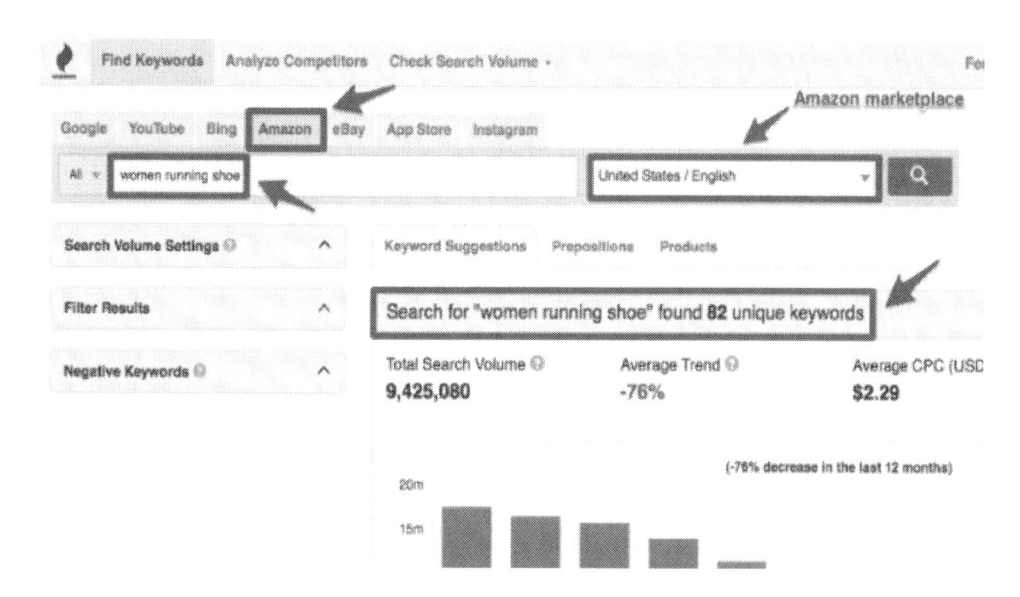

Picture 24

As you can see, all you need to do is type into the search bar the kind of product you are selling, select your location, marketplace language where you intend to sell, and you'll be presented with a summary based on a 12-month average cost-per-click trend for Amazon ads, and what the average competition level is for a specific keyword. Scroll downwards from the screen above and Amazon will even present you with a list of related keywords to match like so:

Keywords	Search Volume	Trend	CPC (USD)	Competition
women running shoe	2,232,000	-70%	$2.81	1.00 (High)
women running shoes	2,232,000	-76%	$2.81	1.00 (High)
women running shoe nike	1,225,000	-75%	$1.84	1.00 (High)
nike women running shoes	1,225,000	-75%	$1.84	1.00 (High)
asics women running shoes	998,000	-87%	$2.16	1.00 (High)
women running shoes brooks	672,000	-76%	$1.81	1.00 (High)
adidas women running shoes	368,000	-55%	$2.16	1.00 (High)
new balance women running shoes	300,000	-70%	$1.83	1.00 (High)
women running shoe puma	59,800	-64%	$1.57	1.00 (High)
women running shoes reebok	39,900	-65%	$2.89	1.00 (High)
women running shoes on sale	32,700	0%	$2.52	1.00 (High)
women running shoes pink	21,800	-80%	$1.79	1.00 (High)
women running shoes overpronation	8,000	-64%	$3.11	1.00 (High)
women running shoes 8.5	8,000	-92%	$3.24	1.00 (High)

Picture 25

The keyword tool is very useful, and you should aim to run a keyword search before listing every product you intend to sell.

There is a wealth of information that you can get which will make a difference to your rankings. You are not just gaining insight into what relevant or trending keywords you should be using, but more importantly, you are getting a firsthand insight into the kind of products your customers (and potential customers) are keen on. Ads, an optimized website and the use of specific keywords has the potential to drive more traffic to your store and convert more customers daily. Your objective, then, is to get more traffic to your site so that it can generate a good percentage of sales. SEO can help drive long-term sales simply by having you rank high on search engine results.

Besides SEO optimization, other things you can do to improve your visibility and rankings include:

- **Provide Excellent Customer Service -** Do not just rely on Amazon to handle your customer service. Take the initiative to go the extra mile by following up with the customer directly. People will *always* remember the way that you made them feel, the experience that you provided. Offering great customer service is one of the best ways to stand out especially if you are selling the same products as every merchant out there. Going the extra mile can be in the form of thank you cards included in the shipping packages, or it could even be a gift! A speedy response to their issues or complaints will go a long way too. Whatever you do, make your customers feel valued and appreciated - it is because of them that you are a success.

- **Coming Up with Fantastic Deals** - Hardly any consumer is ever able to resist a good deal. Sales, bundles, and offers are something almost *every consumer* love! Running these fantastic offers on your page will not only make you noticeable but also increases traffic to your site. If no products on your site are for sale, customers visiting your site will lack the motivation to purchase your products. However, the right product with the right offer to sweeten the deal will only increase the likelihood of them making a purchase. A good tip would be to run these offers during a special celebration or holiday festive season, which gives them even more reason to buy it from you.

- **Be an Active Seller** - It is off-putting to a customer to see a store that has not been updated in months. They will even begin to wonder if your store is operational anymore. While you do not need to spend eight hours a day working on markcting and promoting your site, you still need to commit several hours daily to ensure that your store is up to date, relevant and active.

- **Optimize It with A Website -** Amazon FBA should not be your only selling platform alone, you still have to have an eCommerce website to establish a stronger presence. Somewhere your customers can go to find out more information about you. WordPress, Wix, and Squarespace have made it easy to quickly set up a site in a matter of minutes. For the sake of visibility, it is crucial that your site is optimized. *Crucial.* Let us say customer types into the Google search bar an item that they are looking for, and that item happens to be in your store. How will they find it if Google or any other search engine fails to detect it enough to bring it to their attention? Customers cannot buy what they do not know exists.

- **Proper Page Titles -** The right kind of page titles can do wonders for an optimal site listing. Your page titles must correspond to the products you are selling, and it needs to be attention grabbing enough to boost click-through rates. Do not forget about including keywords into the page title too, and a good tip would be to try to place the main keyword right at the front of the title.

- **Include Unique Meta Descriptions for Your Items** - While keywords added into the meta descriptions on your site don't do much to affect the rankings, you should still include them anyway, because it can still drive traffic to your page. The best use of meta descriptors is to explain what is available on your page and give your customers all the information that they are looking to get before deciding on a purchase. Make it unique, but not too lengthy. Push forth the key selling points of the product to boost click-through rates, and use numbers, prices and other formatting options to make your product stand out.

- **Paying Attention to Your Product's URLs -** URLs are sometimes the least considered optimization element. Clean and keyword-friendly URLs make a huge impact on search rankings. If you have old URLs, make sure they are redirected to the new URLs on your site. Your URLs must be user- friendly and appear directly beneath the title in search engine results. Again, these URLs must be short and written all in lowercase, they must include keywords too.

How to Get More Product Reviews

Product reviews are an ultimate must for a site. It builds trust and enables user engagement as well. When enabling product reviews for your site, make sure that the text is crawl-able. You need variety on your reviews too and sometimes not all of them are going to be five-star reviews, but that is okay. Some sellers are reluctant to approve of negative reviews and feedback, preferring to delete them instead to give the impression that their store is nothing short of fantastic. That approach may have worked in the past, but customers have caught onto it now and they are not easily fooled.

A shop with nothing but great reviews that sound too good to be true arouses suspicion. If you want to get more product reviews in, you need to show that you are a business who cares about honesty, transparency, and trust. Varied feedback gives your product a more legitimate reputation and foothold to stand on. One way of turning negative reviews into positive results is to promptly respond to the feedback and let the customer - *along with all the other customers who are reading the reviews* - see just how quickly and proactively you try to appease the customers' concerns. Offer solutions, problem-solve and be transparent about your communication.

For customers who have made a purchase, encourage them to leave reviews on your site by following up with them or offering an incentive for them to share their honest opinion (regardless if it is good or bad). Like a 5% discount voucher to share their thoughts and sales experience. Other methods of attaining more customer reviews consistently would be to:

- Provide excellent customer service of course. Make the customers extremely happy with their shopping experience and they will be more than happy to leave a quick review.
- You also need to sell good quality products that customers regularly purchase. Regular purchases mean regular reviews.

- Use emails to follow-up with your customers, but do not make it one of those generic, boring, standardized email. Add a personal touch, as if you are speaking to a friend, and ask them if they would not mind sharing their thoughts.

- Reach out to your customers via social media and ask them to share their comments or leave a quick thought about what they thought of your products and services.

- Be part of Amazon's Early Reviewer Program, which rewards customers who have already purchased your product to review and share what they thought. Even if they would only give it a one-star rating. In exchange for their time and effort, Amazon then rewards these customers with an Amazon gift card, which could consist of amounts between $1 - $3.

- Use product inserts, which little reminders are written on cards slipped into their packaging that reminds the customers to leave a review once they open the package.

Chapter 5: Keep It Going

Amazon Ads may not be on par just yet with giants Google Ads and Facebook Ads, but they are certainly no slacker in that department either. In 2018 alone, the platform garnered an advertising revenue growth of 250% in its third quarter compared to its 2017 quarter from a year before. With the way Amazon is going, the duopoly giants Google and Facebook could soon find themselves with a third dominating player in the game not too long from now. Amazon is making waves and it has no plans to slow down anytime soon.

Amazon Ads

To be successful at your Amazon advertising efforts, you need a good advertising strategy, which includes:

- **Defining What Your Goals Are -** What do you hope to accomplish out of your FBA business? Brand awareness? Increase in sales numbers after 6 months to a year? Where do you see your business going? Your advertising strategy needs to align your targets and your goals together for best results.

- **Selecting the Best Products for Advertising -** If you are selling several different products on your store, there are some which are going to sell better than others. To leverage the most out of your Amazon Ads, you need to focus on the *most popular* products you have, the ones with the best chance of converting those clicks into actual purchases by the customers. These products should be your best-sellers, competitively priced and always-in stock. These are the ones worth investing your advertising efforts because they draw customers towards your store.

- **Compelling Content -** Keywords and clear descriptions, as mentioned in Chapter 4, are going to play a role in your advertising strategy here too. The details will ultimately convince your customers *why* your product is the one you are looking for. Why they consider ordering from you, and not your competitors. Your details need to be accurate, concise, and easy to read, keyword-rich and let your customers know why it is relevant and why they need it.

Now, let us talk about Amazon Ads and why they matter. When you log onto Amazon, you will type what you are looking for into the search bar at the top of the page using specific keywords relevant to your search, click and wait for the page to load with potential results. At the very top of the page, you will notice some products listed right at the top have the words "Sponsored Post", or maybe even "Ad" next to them. These are Amazon ads.

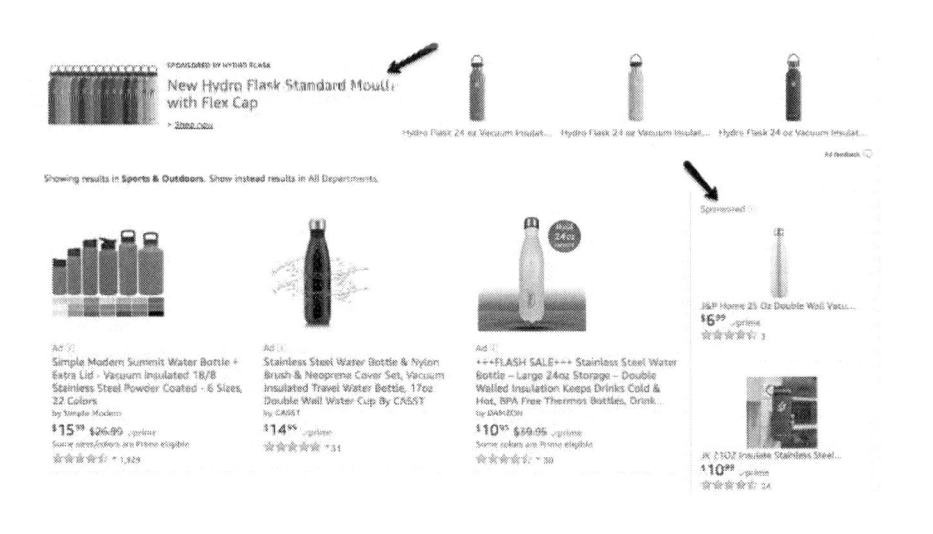

Picture 26

Sellers who want more exposure and visibility for their products have the option of paying them to appear at the very top of the search results. Amazon ads works when you make a payment to Amazon to be positioned at the top by bidding on the specific keyword(s) needed that will increase your visibility on Amazon's Search Engine Results Page (SERP). You will be charged each time a customer clicks on your ad content. To put it simply, Amazon Ads works very much in the same way Google AdWords does.

Amazon Ads can even appear on the product page directly. You could be scrolling for one product and you will see an ad for another product appearing on the side, as you will notice from the image below. Somewhat like scrolling through your News Feed on Facebook and seeing ads pop up at the side enticing you to make a purchase.

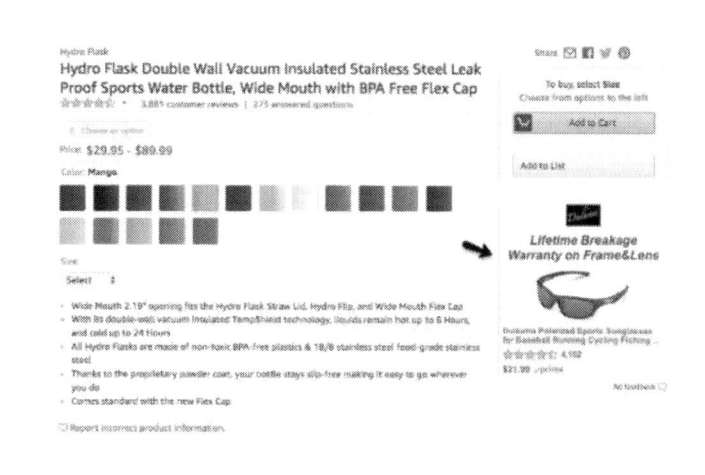

Picture 27

Are Amazon Ads the Best Option for Me?

That would, again, depend on your business goals and what you hope to achieve. If you are selling a product that is tangible, something that your customers can easily purchase online, then yes, Amazon Ads is something you should consider. Particularly in the early stages when you are still trying to get your business off the ground and bring some sales in. Think of it as an additional method of getting your products in front of the right customers, on top of your already existing marketing efforts. More exposure is always better for business.

If you have your reservations in the beginning (you want to try it out, but you are not sure if it is going to work), try starting out with a smaller product first. Something you already know sells quickly and is popular among customers. Perhaps something you would buy yourself. Start with your best-selling product (if you've been selling for a while that is), or if you've just started, do a little digging into what some of Amazon's best-selling merchandise are and see if any of it is like yours. That should give you a good idea of where to start.

Invest in advertising for your bestseller, and once the return on investment from that product starts coming in with the ad, you can think about expanding to promote other products that you want to sell. Amazon ads are great if you are hoping to give your organic search rankings a boost too, especially if you are going with the Amazon PPC option. Keywords that are used in Amazon's PPC ads will considerably boost your organic search rankings, thanks to the extra sales that keep coming in because of those ads. Your store's sales history is going to play a big part in where you end up on the search results page too. Products which sell better are favored by Amazon and placed higher on the search results ranking.

To start using Amazon's ad services, you will need to have an Amazon seller's account. Alternatively, a vendor's account works fine too. First-party sellers might prefer to sign-up on Amazon as a vendor, but this is an invite-only type of situation. If you are selling through the Seller Central, you are a third-party seller. The Seller Central has a few pricing options you can work with. There is an option to pay as you go for those who are selling independently and a pro option if you are selling at a higher volume.

Get started advertising your products

Log in to get started advertising your products

I have a seller account
I have a vendor account
I don't have a seller or vendor account yet

Picture 28

Amazon Ad Types

Once again, Amazon has provided options for you to choose from, so you can go with the one that suits your business needs the best. There is a reason why they are the best out there when it comes to eCommerce and retail, and having some options that cater to everyone's needs is one of them. There are three types of Amazon ads to choose from, depending on what you may need:

Sponsored Ad Options

If you are familiar with how Google's Shopping Network works, this one is similar. Sponsored ads drive your customers directly to the exact products that you happen to be selling on your FBA store. By clicking on the sponsored content, customers will be led directly to your store, complete with the product details and everything else they need to know before they make a purchase.

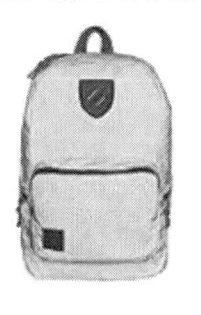

Ad ⓘ

Imperial Motion Group Fillmore Reflective Backpack
by Imperial Motion Group

$59⁹⁵ ✓prime (4-5 days)
Some sizes/colors are Prime eligible

Ad ⓘ

High Sierra Swerve Backpack
by High Sierra

$42⁹⁹ ✓prime
Some colors are Prime eligible

Picture 29

You will typically find these sponsored contents either above or at the bottom of the search results page, once you have typed in the keyword and hit the search button. Sponsored content relies on keywords to hit its targets, and if this is the option you choose to go with, you'll need to have an exact keyword, phrase and several other matching keyword options ready. Sponsored content allows you to have full control regarding how long you want your campaign to run, and the daily budget you set for yourself. You can choose to pause your campaign at any time, but you need to at least let it run for one full day before you do that.

Headline Search Ads

These ads appear as a banner above the results page.

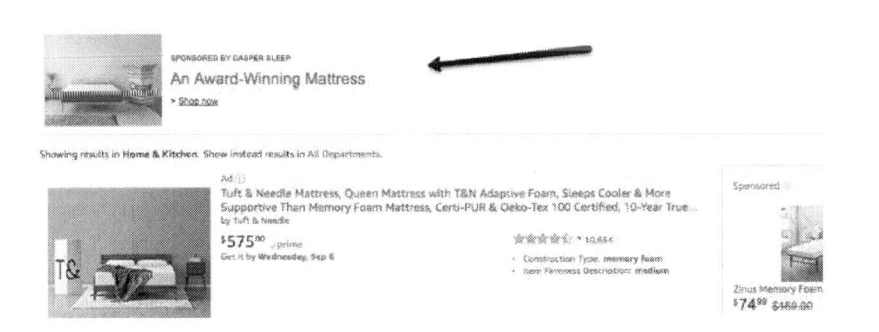

Picture 30

These ads work on a cost-per-click system, leading your customers to the specific page on Amazon that they might be looking for. The minimum bid that you would need to pay per keyword is $0.10. Just like the sponsored content, these ads rely heavily on keywords. The difference with headline ads is that they can be used to promote either three products or more simultaneously. With this ad type, these are only two keyword match-types, which are supported:

- Using the exact keywords
- Using phrases that match

You can schedule your campaigns to run for up to 4 months at a time if you would like and if you have the budget for it.

Product Displays

This ad type works a little differently from the two formats mentioned above. Unlike the other two ad types, this one is not so focused on the keywords. Instead, product display ad formats are based on the product or interest in the targeted ads. Customers are taken to the products page with all the details listed when they click on the ad content.

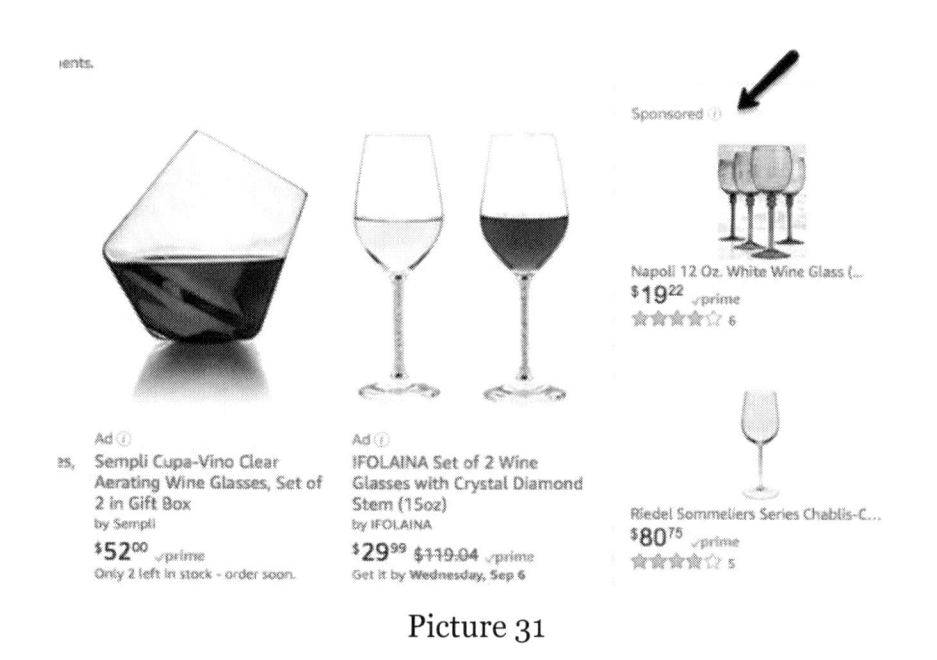

Picture 31

If you choose to go with this approach, you will need to have a long product list to choose from or products of interest. For example, if your target audience was women who were interested in running, then your targeted products would be focused on the running gear you sell or any other items of interest that are related to running and exercise. These ads will then be displayed to customers who are interested in your products. These ads also work on a cost-per-click system, but each campaign is only limited to a single target type.

Product display ads can either appear at the bottom of the page below the search results, at the top of an offer listings page, marketing emails sent out by Amazon, and even on pages where customers leave a review.

Optimizing Your Amazon Ads

Deciding to go ahead with an Amazon ad campaign alone is not enough. You are going to have to optimize that approach for success too. Remember that you are not going to be the only retailer on the platform, there is going to be a lot - *A LOT* - of competition. Literally thousands of other stores and retailers that you will be competing with. There is very little chance of you being seen, let alone being remembered if you do not do what you can to optimize every strategy you take. You need to give your business its best chance for success, and that includes what you do on your Amazon ad campaigns.

Here are the strategies you need to keep in mind if you are serious about taking your Amazon ads to the next level:

- **Campaigns That Are Well-Structured -** If you have had any experience advertising with AdWords in the past, then you are probably familiar with what this process entails. A well-structured campaign works best if you have a separate campaign per product category instead of trying to group everything all together. Once you have sorted out what your campaigns should be, create specific ad groups which are more detailed, narrowing it down even more. A well-structured ad campaign is organized and, more importantly, it remains relevant.

- **Be Compelling in Your Copy -** Create a sense of urgency too, while you are at it. Being detailed in your ad copy does not mean you have to be boring. Go ahead, add some humor in there, and show off your creativity, because it makes your ad copy a lot more compelling. Customers do not want to feel as though they are reading from a generic and dry script. They will remember you a lot more if you made them laugh or smile while they read your product descriptions, and that is one of the most effective ways to stand out on Amazon against a sea of other retailers selling the same thing you are. Creating a sense of urgency in your ad copy here can be through a limited time offer sale, or a not-to-be-missed promotion.

- **Details Matter -** Paying attention to detail is going to be your ad campaign's redeeming quality. Put yourself in your customers' shoes. How convinced would you be about buying a product when you are not satisfied it has answered all your questions. The ad campaigns could be beautifully set up, yet you are not convinced enough because it still feels like something is missing. That is the feeling you want to *avoid* creating for your customers. Detail, detail, detail. That is the mantra you need to keep repeating to yourself when you are prepping for your ad campaign. No matter what product you may be selling, put all the details out there, especially the ones that many sellers sometimes overlook. Even if you are selling something as simple as a water bottle, go the extra mile and put in the nitty-gritty details. How many ounces does this bottle hold? Is it BPA free? Will it keep your beverage cold or hot? If so, for how many hours? What is the material of the water bottle made of? You have limited space on your ad text to work with, so draft out the first copy with *all* the information on it, and then draft out a second copy narrowing it down to *only the most important* information.

- **Consider Your Competitors -** Depending on the kind of product you are selling, think about who your more well-known direct competitors are. The ones who are selling products similar to yours. Let us say for example you were selling workout gear, so you will want to bid on terms such as "Nike sports shoes" or "Adidas socks" for example. Yes, they are not your products, but these well-known brand names are what commonly appear in the search results the most when customers are looking for products like these to purchase. Bidding on the same terms that your competitors are using will allow you to gain some much-needed exposure on Amazon, and give you a small window of opportunity why customers should be buying from you instead of them.

- **Experimenting with The Different Formats -** It is worth trying out all three of Amazon's ad offerings to see which one ends up yielding the most return on investment for your business. Sponsored ad content might seem like it is enough to get the job done, but you just might be surprised at how well the other two formats can work too. A business is always going to be a learning process, one that is constantly evolving and changing. What works well now, might not work as well a year from now, and you are going to have to adapt as you go along.

Mistakes to Avoid

Moving onto some of the blunders and pitfalls that you want to try to avoid when you are just starting out on your Amazon FBA venture. There's nothing worse than pouring your heart into your business, only to have it quickly derail because of one, two or several mistakes that completely unravel all the weeks and months of hard work you may have put in. Nobody likes making mistakes, but, when you are running a business, they are part of the package. While you may not be able to avoid them entirely, what you *can do* is minimize the mistakes you make by learning from the experiences of others. Alternatively, following the advice guidelines below:

- **Mistake 1 - Not Sticking to Your Word.** If you promise something on your store, listing or website, you should better believe the customer is going to hold you to your word. When you promise fast delivery, you need to live up to that promise, along with any other guarantees or assurances you have made to sweeten the deal. Not sticking to your word is the surest way to drive a customer away for good. Before you promise, make sure you can deliver on that promise.

- **Mistake 2 - Confusing Return Policies.** Despite your best efforts, sometimes a customer simply is not happy and wants to return an item that they ordered. You're bound to encounter a customer or two eventually who will want to return what they've bought, and one mistake a lot of newbie entrepreneurs tend to make is not having a clear enough returns policy in place. Dealing with refunds can be a hassle, but with a clear returns policy in place, you can help your buyers make an informed decision *before* they purchase your product. Should they then want to return it, everyone is clear about what the process is going to entail. Overlooking this aspect is only going to create an unpleasant sales experience both ways because of the time-consuming and tedious back and forth that needs to go on before you and the client can come to an understanding.

- **Mistake 3 - Not Spending Enough Time on Listings.** Without quality listings in place, you are not giving your buyer a compelling enough reason why they should choose you over your competitors. In the rush to put their products up for sale, a lot of new sellers gloss over this aspect by just providing the bare minimum information and hope that is going to be enough to suffice. It is not.

- **Mistake 4 - Not Taking Note of Changes in Policy.**
We are all guilty of scrolling through the terms and
conditions and clicking "accept" without reading any of it.
Who does have the time for that? Well, you are going to
need to, if you are running a business. At least read and
thoroughly understand any new changes or updates in
their policy, which Amazon sends you. These changes
could affect your business, so it is best you try to be as
thorough as you can and do not skip this step.

- **Mistake 5 - Your Wait Times Are Too Long.**
Customers are an impatient bunch. Take too long to
deliver and they will go to someone else to get the job done.
It is not just the long wait times for the delivery of their
product that is going to drive them away either. If you take
too long to respond to their queries, too long to restock
your inventory, too long resolve return issues, providing a
slow overall sales experience in general, the customer is
going to take their business elsewhere and it is going to be
nearly impossible to win them back.

- **Mistake 6 - Limited Logistics.** Servicing within your
own country, continent or region is certainly easier and a
lot more convenient, but there is the danger of missing
potential customers too. The international market is where

153

an even bigger customer potential lies, and at some point, you are going to have to think about servicing that sector for the future of your business.

- **Mistake 7 - Slacking Off.** You will have to work your butt off until your business gets to the point where you can call it a success. There is a steady stream of revenue coming in every month, and you are getting plenty of great reviews and returning customers too. It is easy to get comfortable, but the danger is when you start to get a little *too* comfortable that your performance starts to slip. To keep your success going, you need to keep the momentum you built going, and falling behind on your performance should never even be an option.

- **Mistake 8 - More Than One Account.** Amazon is only going to let you register for a single account, and nothing more. All you get is one, and another mistake made by many new entrepreneurs is trying to set up multiple accounts for themselves, thinking they will boost sales even more. Unfortunately, going that way is going to put you in violation of Amazon's policies, and they will be well within their legal rights to either terminate or suspend your account.

- **Mistake 9 - Too Much Inventory That is Not Moving.** This mistake usually hits the new sellers more than the seasoned ones. Understandable, since this is probably your first time doing it, and you are not quite sure how much stock you need to have on hand. It is going to take a while for you to find that balance between having the perfect amount of inventory, so until then, try to pace yourself with your ordering, do your research and be realistic about how much you are going to need.

- **Mistake 10 - Sorry, Out of Stock.** Unfortunately, sorry is not going to be enough to pull your customers back in once they have moved onto another seller. Customers are a fickle bunch, and even if they have bought from your store in the past, they can quickly lose interest when faced with an "out of stock" situation. As a seller, you never want to have to tell your customers that an item is out of stock, which is why having software to help you manage your inventory is going to be a great solution in this case.

- **Mistake 11 - Failing to Deliver.** The whole idea of having "fulfilled by Amazon" stamped across the products in your store is because customers have come to expect dependability and reliability. That is what they associate Amazon with, and things as order cancellations or delays

155

in shipment can seriously damage your reputation. True, there are times when circumstances are beyond your control, but letting Amazon handle the shipping and handling aspect of it instead of trying to do it yourself helps minimize instances of failed order fulfillment.

- **Mistake 12 - Thinking eBay Rules Apply to Amazon.** Selling experience on eBay is going to help you in some ways, but not entirely. Amazon and eBay have many similarities between them but make no mistake they are two different platforms. The rules do not apply across the board, and what works on eBay might not work the same way on Amazon. Keep the two accounts separate, and learn to understand and familiarize yourself with the different nuances that set Amazon apart.

- **Mistake 13 - Your Shipping Costs Too Much.** There are times when a slightly higher shipping rate is to be expected (like when you are expediting the shipping, or rushing an order, maybe even having it shipped to a remote location that is hard to access). However, if the cost of the shipping exceeds more than 20% of what the item itself costs, customers are not going to be happy about it. High shipping costs are a major turn-off, so you need to figure out how much your base selling cost should be if you want to make a reasonable profit, which will then allow you to cut down on the shipping costs as much as possible.

- **Mistake 14 - Not Following Up with Reviews.** Remember how reviews are important to the survival of your business? Well, one mistake that too frequently is made is sellers forget to follow-up with their customers and prompt them to leave a review. Once customers get what they want, they do not think twice about it anymore, and leaving a review is not something that will even cross their minds at that point. Which is why you need to make it a point to remind them (without being too pushy about it) by following up and asking them to share their experience.

- **Mistake 15 - Stagnant Prices.** Customers always want to know that they are getting a good deal. They take advantage of sales, special offers and price reductions, especially when prices are slashed at nearly 50%. As a seller, it would be a mistake to always keep your product prices stagnant, since the minute your competitor lowers their prices, customers are going to immediately jump the fence over to the other side.

- **Mistake 16 - Trying to Add External URLs.** You might have other stores on different platforms or even your own eCommerce store that you are eager to drive traffic towards, but trying to add on external URLs within your product listing is going against Amazon's policy.

- **Mistake 17 - Messy Images.** Keep your product images simple, clean and crisp, with not a lot of detail going on that you end up confusing your customers. The background of your chosen image should not distract from the actual product you are trying to sell. If it does, you have gone too far and you will need to tone it down.

Even More Tips and Tricks for Success on Amazon

As an FBA seller, you need all the help you can get to ensure your business on Amazon runs like a well-oiled machine. Do not overlook the available tools at your disposal, especially if you are a multi-channel seller. There is no shortage of tools these days available to help you out in just about every aspect of running an FBA store, as a quick Google search will reveal. One drawback though is that some of these tools can be a little on the pricey side, and as a new entrepreneur, you are probably still in the budget-conscious stage of your business. But then again, even well-seasoned businesses might hesitate to sign up for an app where you are uncertain if it meets your business needs. Luckily, most of them come with trial periods so you can test it out and see if it works for you.

When these tools come free though, it does not hurt to invest in them; especially if they can help you elevate your game. Here is a list of some of the free Amazon tools that make searching for products easier, identify what is new in the market, and even tools that work great at giving you updates, tips, and advice. The best part being, of course, that they are free.

- **AMZFinder** - This powerful review and feedback management tool are a definite must-have for Amazon sellers. Create auto-email plans, and gain access to 500 free emails a month to optimize your listings and increase your revenue. There is also a transparent pricing system in place, as well as a resourceful blog section that is updated regularly with informational articles, product comparisons, and advice on just about any aspect of Amazon.

- **AMZBase** - Take your product search speed up a notch by using AMZBase, the free Amazon product search tool. AMZBase lets you get a hold of product ASIN numbers as well as effective product descriptions and it gives quick access to plenty of sites directly from the menu.

- **<u>Camelcamelcamel</u>** - Created by Daniel Green, this platform offers a host of information and resources that are extremely valuable for any Amazon FBA seller, even if you are a more seasoned pro. You will need to go through a quick and short registration process but after that, it is completely free to access. There are no other charges incurred if you want access to tutorials and downloads. There is a tools section too, which features free add-ons as well as downloads, and there is a guide to price drops and popular products. Users have free access to view Amazon history charts and sign up for alerts. The platform has also included a useful sales rank and price history data feature that sellers are going to find very useful.

- **<u>Keepa</u>** - This Amazon price-tracking tool has its benefits. Created by Sascha Arthur, may not be as robust as some of the tools used, but plenty of Amazon sellers find it useful as a browser extension because it includes an Amazon price tracker as well as a "Deals" section, which regularly highlights popular products and products that have a price drop.

- **Sonar** - This Chrome extension is best utilized for Amazon keyword research. Using complex algorithms and collating data on the products that shoppers on Amazon are searching for, Sonar puts it in together into a database. This is an ideal tool for those who have not decided what it is they would want to sell. This is also an excellent generator for ideas. Users find this tool effective, it also includes options to optimize back end keywords, and it gives users the capacity to develop their own profit dashboard.

- **Google Trends** - Simple but effective. Google Trends will let you keep up to date on all-important trends happening in the business. This is also an essential FBA tool that sellers need to have, as it gives an overview list of the list of trending stories, along with its historical data, which gives sellers a bird's eye view of what is trending and what is not. It also has an online search option that enables sellers to search for products and subjects that may not appear on the access and list data. What is great about Google Trends is that it is updated daily and it is an excellent site to put in your favorites list and stay on top of what is trending on a minute-to-minute basis.

- **Keyword Tool for Amazon** - A tool that helps Amazon sellers easily search for a specific keyword, this is one feature you want to make full use of. It is still free to use, even if you do not register, and through this platform, users get to put in a 750 long-tail keyword suggestion for every search item. You can search in YouTube, Bing, Google, eBay, Amazon, and even App store and you can filter it by country. This tool, while basic is still a great tool to keep on your browser for easy and quick searches.

- **DS Amazon Quick View** - Another Chrome extension that is quick and easy to install, this productivity tool will allow you to add an Amazon ranking, and provide information to check on full product details effortlessly. It is free to install, but there are going to be fees incurred if you need some help and support. To avoid the fees, you can opt to visit forums for any troubleshooting issues you may have.

- **FBA Calculator** - Another tool that was previously talked about was the FBA Calculator for Amazon. Calculate profit margins faster while on the move, anytime you need with the FBA Calculator. You can get it free from the Chrome store and users can estimate profits on any given product and see its cost price, estimated sales as well as the number of variables.

- **<u>Unicorn Smasher</u>** - This unique sounding tool is considered among the best ways to supercharge your product research on Amazon. It is a colorful website, true to its name, with tons of useful downloads, statistics, information, and reports. Through this tool users can integrate AMZ tracker and it offers plenty of features from fulfillment details, monthly estimates, export tools, revenue estimates as well as data analysis.

Even More Secrets to Success to Amazon FBA Success. If Other Sellers Can Do It, You Can Too

Not secrets exactly, but more like things you *NEED* to do if you want to achieve all the success on Amazon that you hoped for when you had that first spark of inspiration to start this venture. Many sellers make the mistake of either overlooking or ignoring the little details. You do not want to be one of those sellers who is so eager to get going you rush through the entire process and end up making several mistakes along the way. It is the little details that will lead to overall success, not merely buying and selling inventory alone. Many other things go into it.

Let us look at some of little details you should be paying attention to:

- **Optimizing Your Page for Mobile Viewing** - Mobile phones these days are designed for us to have information in the palm of our hands and on the go. Any content you create today must be optimized for mobile viewing first and desktop second. This includes your Amazon FBA store (and other eCommerce stores you have). Customers are more likely to view your newsletters, product updates, emails, statutes, and tweets via mobile than on their desktop, and if your store is not optimized for mobile viewing, you are already on the losing end.

- **Optimal Pricing Is a Must** - Every customer who goes to Amazon to purchase something often wants to buy products at the lowest price. No exceptions here. If you can get what you needed for a much lower cost, of course you would want to. As a seller, you need to think like your customer. You need to know the kind of prices that you will be competing against, and how to sell your products at the most optimal, competitive pricing. Items that are priced lower show up higher on the search results but be careful that it is not too low. Your pricing needs to be competitive and to do that, you can use Amazon's Match Low Price feature to assist you in consistently matching with the lowest pricing of the same product on Amazon.

- **You Need the Buy Box** - The Amazon Buy Box is the Holy Grail sellers strive to achieve. Located on the product detail page where customers start the purchasing process by adding items directly into their shopping cart, products listed here often see an increase in purchases.

- **Always Improve, Never slack** - Remember how you need to keep the same performance and standard going? Even when you have achieved steady success on Amazon? Using Amazon FBA means your packaging, shipping, and even customer service are handled by Amazon, but it does not mean you do not get to do anything else. Your job is to make sure your store is continuously selling and to do this, you need to consistently improve your store's performance and monitor it regularly. You need to be mindful of the sales, the seller rating as well as the return rates. You got your store to the top of its game, now you need to help it stay there.

- **Never Neglect the Reviews** - The best way for any customer to know that the products that they are purchasing are good value is by reading the reviews.

Customers will click on products that have higher ratings and the likelihood of them finalizing purchases increases if products have good reviews and high ratings. Never give in to the temptation to cheat on your reviews. If you have a product that always gets bad, reviews- trash it. When you do, let your customers know that you are discontinuing it because this will help increase their confidence in your site. The fact that you have heard them and you are doing something about it increases brand trust.

- **Following Amazon's Rules** - Success does not come by cutting corners. Even if you do by some luck, you are not going to stay there for long. You can take advantage of tools and apps that help you be more efficient and up to date. Nevertheless, the golden rule here is to follow the rules set by Amazon and your account will not be penalized or suspended.

- **Detailed Image Views-** You want to entice customers to purchase your products. Apart from a single photo, give users views from different angles as it can show character and carry a brand. Provide thoughtful and visually appealing imagery, and do not just show your products from one angle either. Always have a few different angles and views, with some zooming in on the finer details.

Images are also a way your customer gathers information. If they love what they see, they will buy it. Purchasing stock photos is not as effective these days. Customers want to see the real deal where possible. If you are running your own eCommerce store, genuine pictures highlighting the lifestyle of your company, your employees, the surrounding of your firm is a hundred times better than regular stock photos.

- **System Integration for Efficiency** - Integration allows you to synchronize various data such as orders, inventory, customers, items as well as shipping and tracking information between your other systems and Amazon. If you are on other channels, make it a point to integrate your sales channels with your backend systems. You can automate these processes and eliminate manual data entry, which can cause delayed data processing time as well as errors that are costly.

Conclusion

Thank for making it through to the end of this book, let us hope it was informative and able to provide you with all the tools you need to achieve your goals whatever they may be.

Amazon FBA can be a great place to start an online eCommerce business or an excellent addition to your already existing retail business. Novice sellers get to learn what it takes to run an online store without having to bear the burden of a massive risk that might land them in debt. The Amazon team is there to help you every step of the way, from the payments to the packaging, shipping and even dealing with your customer service, which is why it is the perfect passive income option. Minimal work on your part, but still good enough to generate a recurring income, even when you are not actively working on it yourself.

The name *Amazon* will take your business further than you ever thought possible, connecting you to a wide range of customers globally. Like most business models, Amazon does come with its own pros and cons, but once you start getting into the business yourself, you'll see firsthand that the pros far outweigh the cons, making this business model worth it. Many sellers have already found success on Amazon by either increasing their sales or boosting the visibility of their existing stores by branching out into Amazon FBA. You could be one of those sellers too.

Finally, if you found this book useful in any way, a review on Amazon is always appreciated!

By the same Author:

Made in the
USA
Columbia, SC